FLESH AND BLOOD
FAMILICIDES AND MURDER-SUICIDES
THAT HAUNT IRELAND

Nicola Tallant is Investigations Editor with the *Sunday World*. She has written extensively about crime in Ireland over the past sixteen years. She holds a Higher Diploma in Criminology.

FLESH AND BLOOD

Familicides and Murder-Suicides that Haunt Ireland

Nicola Tallant

HACHETTE
BOOKS
IRELAND

First published in 2011 by Hachette Books Ireland

1

A CIP catalogue record for this title is available from the British Library.

ISBN 978 1 444 70768 7

Typeset in Sabon by Hachette Books Ireland
Printed and bound in Great Britain by CPI Mackays, Chatham ME5 8TD

Hachette Books Ireland policy is to use papers that are natural, renewable and recyclable products and made from wood grown in sustainable forests. The logging and manufacturing processes are expected to conform to the environmental regulations of the country of origin.

Front jacket images clockwise from top left: The Fox family; Diarmuid and Lorraine Flood; the McElhill family; the Dunne family.
Back jacket images clockwise from top left: Deirdre Crowley; Greg Fox; Sharon Grace; Mikahla and Abby Grace.

203868
€14

Hachette Books Ireland
8 Castlecourt Centre
Castleknock
Dublin 15, Ireland
A division of Hachette UK Ltd
338 Euston Road
London NW1 3BH

www.hachette.ie

CONTENTS

INTRODUCTION

They are the stories that haunt us, that force us to dig deep into our souls for sympathy, and shock us to the core. Yet they take place in Ireland, in seemingly happy homes and in inexplicable moments of apparent madness.

For years, academics have tried to explain these cases, which are so rare that surely we shouldn't know of any worthy of our interest. And yet we do – and over the past decade we have heard about too many parents who have turned on their own flesh and blood. Familicide, filicide and murder-suicide have become all too familiar in Ireland. So called 'family wipeouts' have left their indelible images on the collective conscience of the nation. Nothing will explain conclusively why a man or woman chose to murder his or her own family.

Across the globe, familicide – the killing of an entire family followed by the suicide of the perpetrator – is recognised as principally a male phenomenon. The killer has often been profiled as a good family man, a loyal husband and father who is consumed by a sense of inadequacy. He is tipped over the edge by something that makes him feel he is losing control over those he considers he owns: his children and wife or partner.

But familicide is not exclusively male. In the natural order it is a mother's role to nurture and provide for her child and – in certain circumstances – even to give her own life for her son or daughter. There are few things that society deems more unnatural and terrifying than a mother who kills her child. What, in the end, drives a woman to take that young life?

For a long time in Ireland, mental illness was hidden, the secret shame of many families. It may, or may not, lie behind at least some of these appalling crimes. It is difficult to sympathise with a killer. It is almost impossible to empathise with a child killer – particularly when he or she is, or was, a parent. But to understand what forces a parent to kill, or a husband to murder the wife he once loved, and perhaps still loves, we must leave behind our prejudices and walk with them into their darkness.

1

IF I CAN'T HAVE YOU . . .
The Cases of Greg Fox, Stephen Byrne, George McGloin and James Byrne

The scenes of savagery that greeted those who first entered Debbie and Greg Fox's comfortable bungalow home on a bright summer morning in July 2001 were so horrific and gruesome that they will remain firmly etched on their minds for the rest of their lives. 'If there was ever a hell on earth, it was in that blood-drenched house. Its interior bore more of a resemblance to the inside of a busy abattoir than a family home,' one seasoned detective told the *Sunday World*.

It was a Saturday in the sleepy village of Castledaly in Westmeath and the shutters remained down on the Foxes' grocery, adjacent to the home that the young couple had moved to just eighteen months before, so that they could bring up their children in a safe rural environment. Those who came to buy their papers, their milk or fill their car at one of the four pumps at the front couldn't understand why the shop hadn't opened for business as usual, and why Greg and his pretty wife Debbie weren't behind the counter. The curtains at the windows of their small bungalow remained drawn and those who knocked got no response. As the morning wore on, neighbours became suspicious and called gardaí to come and investigate.

The peace and innocence of the tiny village was shattered that warm summer morning when officers used a hammer to break a window and made their way inside. There they discovered dark-haired Debbie's broken and battered body in a pool of blood on the kitchen floor. The bodies of her sons Trevor, nine, and Killian, seven, were mutilated in their separate bedrooms. They had been repeatedly stabbed with a butcher's knife. Their father, Greg, was discovered lying on the floor: he had slashed his wrists.

Just a few hours earlier, Fox – he would later be described as a domineering bully who wanted to control every aspect of Debbie's life – had embarked on a crazed attack on his family. He had repeatedly punched Debbie in the face, so hard that she had collapsed onto a table laden with bottles of drink. He had then grabbed a broken Budweiser bottle, stabbed her in the neck and banged her head off the kitchen floor. Then he got a kitchen knife and stuck it into her chest and throat.

But Fox still wasn't finished. He went out to a storeroom, got a hurl and a long-handled butcher's knife and, as his wife of eleven years lay dying on the floor, he beat her over the head with the hurl, fracturing her skull.

Satisfied that she was dead, he headed upstairs with the butcher's knife to where his two little boys lay sleeping. He stabbed them forty-seven times. Trevor took the brunt of his father's rage and put up a huge struggle. Stab wounds on his hands would later prove he fought desperately for his life as Fox knifed him thirty-one times. Killian was smaller but he, too, fought back. He was stabbed sixteen times. 'I didn't want the kids to wake up and see their mum like that, so I decided to kill them. I went to the bedrooms and stabbed them,' Fox would later tell officers. 'I loved the three of them. I loved my wife, but she didn't love me. She was going to leave.'

As gardaí cordoned off the house and Technical Bureau officers combed the scene, Deputy State Pathologist Dr Marie Cassidy carried out her preliminary examinations of the bodies before they were removed to Longford Westmeath General Hospital for postmortems. Greg Fox was initially brought to Portiuncula Hospital in Ballinasloe, where his injuries were treated and he was held in a private room manned by gardaí.

But news travelled fast through the village about the horrors that had been discovered inside the Fox home, and there was little sympathy for Greg Fox. Those who had known Debbie were quick to point out that he was obsessive and jealous.

Although they hadn't been living in the village for very long, the Foxes were well-known from their work in the grocery and small filling station that they had bought from local man Sean Kelly. They had told neighbours that they had chosen to settle there for their sons, whom they had enrolled in St Kieran's School a short distance away. Debbie had worked in the shop most days, and was friendly and courteous to those who dropped in for papers or petrol or, in particular during a recent hot spell, for an ice cream. Greg was in and out, often behind the counter, unpacking deliveries or stacking the shelves.

As officers quizzed Fox about his murder spree, rumours circulated of a split in the marriage, and while he was telling gardaí that Debbie had driven him to kill because she was going to leave him, others were saying he was a bully and control freak.

The following Monday he was discharged from hospital and brought to Athlone Garda Station for formal questioning. Outside, a mob gathered, and during the afternoon, officers had to lock the station as tensions increased. Soon 150 people had gathered outside. Later, some screamed abuse at Fox as he was taken, with a coat over his head, from the station to the court. Others rushed the garda barrier, and kicked the car – one man was arrested after Fox had been led into court.

Inside the courtroom, Judge James O'Sullivan heard evidence from Garda Sergeant Sean Leydon about Fox's arrest in relation to the killings. Fox's solicitor Hugh Campbell asked that he be medically assessed in custody and he was remanded to re-appear on 3 August. Throughout the short hearing, he sat in the dock with both arms and his right thumb heavily bandaged; his left arm was in a sling. At times he shook uncontrollably and once almost fell. He stared at the floor for most of the hearing.

Trouble flared again as he left the court.

The following Friday, as the bodies of Debbie and her two young sons were removed to St Killian's Church in Tallaght for burial, Fox was due back in court. He couldn't attend because he was undergoing treatment in the Central Mental Hospital. The chief medical officer at Clover Hill Prison, Dr Noel Browne, told the court that Fox had been assessed by medical staff after he had been remanded and transferred immediately to the Central Mental Hospital in Dundrum. Fox had suffered from injuries to his hands and was now under the care of Dr Harry Kennedy, chief psychiatrist at the Central Mental Hospital. He was not fit to attend court and might not be for some time.

Judge Michael Connellan issued a sick warrant, to be sent to Clover Hill Prison, for Fox to be brought before the court the following Friday; he said he would issue further warrants each week until Fox was fit to appear before the court again. Mr Hugh Campbell, defending, asked that his client receive physiotherapy for his injuries at Tallaght Hospital.

The next day, hundreds of grief-stricken mourners lined out at the church to bid a final farewell to the family Fox had killed in a bloodbath just a week previously. It was the same church where Debbie had married him in 1990. Father Paul O'Driscoll had few words to console those who stared in disbelief at the two white coffins and Debbie's oak one. 'We find ourselves thirsting for consolation,' he said. 'In the depths of our hearts we may well be wondering if there was something we could have done or said to prevent what happened.' All three were buried after the funeral mass at Newlands Cemetery, just around the corner from the church.

At his trial in November 2003, Fox pleaded guilty to the three murders. Looking more like a businessman than a triple killer when he appeared in the dock of Dublin's Central Criminal court, the one-time commercial traveller remained stony-faced as he accepted that he had murdered his wife and two young boys. 'I feel I have caused enough pain to my family and my wife's family, and I do not wish to put everyone through the ordeal of a trial,' he said in a statement.

After his sentencing, it emerged that he and Debbie had spent a night out at the village pub before he had turned into a killer in their house. Debbie's friend Mandy Barrett told the *Irish Mirror* that Fox had moved out of the family home a month before he had killed his young family, as he and Debbie were set to split. She added: 'He decided what makeup she wore and the length of her dresses. I remember one night, a woman friend wanted Debbie to go with her to the cinema to see *Bridget Jones's Diary*. But Greg would not allow her. He said going to the cinema would lead her to go out to pubs, which would lead her to go clubbing, so he stopped her.'

Anyone left with any doubt about the anger and jealous rage that had engulfed Greg Fox that night was in no doubt after the inquest on Debbie and her boys, which took place after his trial. The court heard how many times he had stabbed his little boys after savagely attacking his wife. Deputy State Pathologist Dr Marie Cassidy said all three victims had wounds on their hands, indicating that they had tried to defend themselves against him.

Fox's solicitor read a statement to the inquest in which Fox apologised to the family and expressed remorse. He claimed he never set out to harm his family, but blamed the cataclysmic collapse of his marriage for bringing about a chain of actions that he 'never thought he could be capable of'. County Coroner Dr Wilfred Hoover said Debbie Fox had died of haemorrhage from neck wounds, while Trevor and Killian had died from multiple stab wounds to their faces, necks and trunks. In the courtroom Fox's words of sorrow offered little relief: 'I loved the three of them. I loved my wife so much, but she didn't love me and I just went mad.'

The deaths of little Trevor and Killian Fox in 2001 followed several other child murders in the Republic. Just a year previously, another man's rage at his wife had led him to stab her to death, then to ply his two young sons with alcohol before he drove them off a pier in Wexford. Stephen Byrne sparked an international manhunt when he disappeared in September 2000 with his sons Alan, ten, and six-year-old Shane.

The family had been last seen alive on Monday, 25

September. Stephen, aged forty-one, had attended work at a water-treatment plant while his wife Maeve brought the two boys to their school, De La Salle Primary, in Kilkenny. Two days later, a relative contacted gardaí because he could get no response at the house. When officers arrived there, they discovered Maeve's body in a pool of blood. She had been stabbed with a kitchen knife and was covered with a blanket behind a sofa in the kitchen. Bloodstains indicated that she had been dragged there from where she had been attacked in another part of the room. The ironing board was still standing and two of Stephen's shirts lay neatly folded on a table. Maeve had put up a ferocious struggle for her life but there was no sign of her two boys, Stephen or the family's Wexford-registered white Ford Escort hatchback.

Officers at the scene immediately noted that there were no signs of a break-in and early enquiries indicated that the Byrnes' marriage had been tense because of Maeve's extra-marital affairs. They had moved from Kilkenny to Cuffesgrange to make a new start just two years earlier. From the outset the horrendous attack on Maeve worried officers. Stephen was the chief suspect, but he was missing with the children and they feared for his state of mind. Maeve's body appeared to have lain where it was for at least a couple of days, which meant her husband had probably been on the run ever since. Officers knew they had to catch up with him.

The Garda Technical Bureau was called to the scene although no murder weapons were found. Officially, investigators said they found it difficult to estimate the time of death, but put it somewhere between lunchtime on the Monday and lunchtime on the Wednesday. They wanted as much information, including sightings, from the public as possible and didn't want to state a particular time of death, in case some did not come forward with detail that might prove invaluable.

On the Thursday, Superintendent Kevin Donohue issued a statement saying that, following an overnight postmortem on Mrs Byrne, officers had launched a full murder investigation. 'We are very concerned for the health and safety of Mrs Byrne's husband and her two young sons. Their whereabouts are still unknown,' he said.

The gardaí pulled out all the stops, knowing they were racing against the clock if they were going to catch Byrne and find the little boys alive. They brought in every support available to them, including the garda helicopter and divers, who began searching Waterford Harbour where Byrne had loved to fish. A massive team of officers began combing any possible hiding places near the family home, including isolated barns and outhouses.

Security videos at ports and airports were examined and Interpol were alerted to the possibility that the three had already gone abroad and were somewhere in either the UK or Europe. Pictures of Stephen and the two boys were released across the media and the nation was asked to keep its eyes peeled for them. The public was also urged to help officers by scouring their own properties for signs of anything suspicious. Appeals were made on local radio, and a priest begged Stephen to bring the boys home safely: Father Martin Delaney appeared on *The Pat Kenny Show* to talk about the young family. 'I'm just praying that they will all be found safe and sound,' he said. 'Now I am just hoping that if they are still driving around the area, they will hear these appeals on the car radio and make contact with the police. This is a particularly disturbing and devastating time for their families.' He also made a direct appeal to Stephen: 'This is a devastating kind of blow for a small community like ours. These are not the type of headlines a little village like Cuffesgrange likes to see. It is a very disturbing kind of event. I was saying mass there at nine o'clock and parishioners were particularly struck by the children this morning. They are very conscious of the two boys who are missing. I am very conscious that Stephen has parents, has a father himself – he is a son too – and I am just hoping they are all safe.'

The following morning, as the family of Maeve Byrne were preparing for her burial, two little bodies were washed up on two Wexford beaches. Shane's was found first, on Duncannon beach, by a young mother, Mary McGrath, who was out for an early-morning walk. He was lying face down in seaweed. Two hours later farmer James Power searched the beach near his home after hearing radio reports of the first body being found. As he ran down to the lonely strand on Boyce's Bay, he saw Alan.

Then fishermen spotted the white car in the water off Duncannon Pier as the tide went out. Divers and technical experts managed to lift it from the harbour bed. Initially it was believed that the car would contain the body of the boys' father, but it did not. Forensic experts cordoned off the scenes at the beaches and the pier, while the boys' bodies were taken to Waterford General Hospital for postmortem examination.

News of the grim discoveries reached Foulkstown Cemetery in Kilkenny just moments before Maeve's burial service was due to begin.

At Duncannon Pier people spoke in hushed tones of the madness that had overtaken Stephen Byrne. A keen fisherman, he had taken part in many angling contests in the town, and a ferry operator who worked out of the harbour told journalist Lynne Kelleher that he had taken Stephen out on his boat just two weeks ago. 'He was very nice and very family-orientated. We were late coming in, but all he was concerned about was making sure he rang home so he could say goodnight to his two boys.'

Sergeant Tom Lavery of the Garda Diving Unit had led the search. He said: 'It was very sad. In the back of the car we found hurleys, helmets, a teddy and kids' trainers. The windows were probably smashed with the impact. They were slightly open because the car was upside down in the water. The visibility in the harbour was nil . . . We got a report of three missing people. We've found the boys and we're going to continue to look for the other person. Divers will search around the harbour and there will be searches of the nearby beaches as well. It would have been better for everyone concerned if we had found the body and could bring this investigation to a finish.'

Behind the scenes, officers had pieced together a brief background on the Byrnes' lives. They had married in Kilkenny in 1988 and gone on to have their two children. Stephen was a lorry driver and had worked extensively abroad. Maeve had stayed at home to mind her two children, but two years earlier the couple had moved to Cuffesgrange after she had had a series of affairs. They had decided to give their marriage another go. In recent months, Stephen had begun to suspect his wife was having another affair and they had spoken of splitting up and possibly divorcing. The tension between the couple had evidently ratcheted at some point on that Monday night between nine o'clock and midnight, and Stephen's rage had escalated to a murderous level.

But still Stephen Byrne was missing. The evidence suggested that he had been in the car when it was driven off Duncannon Pier and would have had little chance of survival in the cold and choppy seas. Byrne knew the waters around the harbour and had chosen the deepest spot before he plunged his car headlong over the wall. The vehicle was in gear, the keys in the ignition.

Nearly a week after the brutal murder, Stephen Byrne's tracksuit bottoms were recovered from Boyce's Bay near to where the body of his son Alan had been found. Divers vowed to continue their search, but as the days wore on, the likelihood of finding him became slimmer and slimmer. Five days after the boys had been washed up, searchers concluded that if Byrne was in the water, his body had been swept out to sea. Strong currents in the harbour meant that many drowning victims were never recovered. Three rivers – the Barrow, Nore and Suir – flow into the estuary, producing a raging tide, and experienced searchers warned that once a body had passed Hook Head, it was extremely unlikely to be found.

More than two weeks later, the body of Stephen Byrne was found tangled in trawler nets off the Welsh coast. It was taken to the port of Porthgain in Pembrokeshire, where dental records confirmed its identity.

In December an inquest in Wales heard that Maeve and Stephen Byrne had both been treated for depression. PC Paul Phillips, who had liaised closely with gardaí, said: 'The marriage was strained because Mrs Byrne had been having several affairs. It is known she was having an affair at the time of her death.' He told the inquest in Milford Haven, Pembrokeshire, that she was taking medication in the days before her death. PC Phillips said that Byrne was last seen leaving work at five thirty on the Monday evening and he had phoned his brother Paul a few hours later. When gardaí broke into the family home two days later, they discovered that Maeve had been stabbed three times.

An Irish inquest held in Kilkenny heard the shocking details of how Byrne had given his little boys alcohol before driving them off Duncannon Pier. Deputy State Pathologist Dr Marie Cassidy said that both the boys had a high blood alcohol level before they drowned. But they had been alive when they were driven into the sea. She recorded 35 milligrams of alcohol in ten-year-old Alan's blood but six-year-old Shane's level was even higher at 55 milligrams.

Stephen's brother Paul described how he had found Maeve's body wrapped in a blue sheet in the kitchen. He told Coroner Rory Hogan that he had become worried when his brother failed to ring him. 'On the twenty-ninth of September, myself, my father Mick and my sister Josephine went up to the house with Sergeant Quinlan. Sergeant Quinlan removed the bathroom window as the house was locked up. We were inside for about fifteen to twenty minutes when I noticed a blue towel behind the couch in the kitchen. It was my sister-in-law, Maeve Byrne.'

Dr Cassidy said that the woman's body was face up and had been covered with two blue sheets. A pillow case lay over her head and she was naked underneath a white towelling robe. She believed the body had been dragged behind the couch, as there was bruising on the legs and ankles, and that Mrs Byrne had lain dead in the kitchen for around thirty-six hours before she was discovered. 'She suffered from cardiac trauma and a severe loss of blood. It is not clear if she put up a defence,' she said.

At his conclusion, the coroner said: 'In respect of these tragedies, everybody is greatly saddened, which really is an understatement. The losses and gaps these deaths have left in both families is a great tragedy. On behalf of this court and the gardaí, I would like to extend my sympathies.' No members of either family, except Paul Byrne, had shown up to hear the gruesome findings.

* * *

Stephen Byrne and Greg Fox had killed their own flesh and blood in fits of jealous rage against their partners, but they were not alone in doing so. Four months after Fox had murdered his wife and sons, another man would take out his fury on the woman he could not bear to be without, by killing himself and their little child. George McGloin was a strapping Irish-Canadian who had met Kilkenny girl Lorraine Leahy in 1997. McGloin was a paramedic from Toronto, the son of a former police chief, and a handsome catch.

Lorraine was smitten and moved to Canada with her boyfriend, where she became pregnant. They then moved back to Ireland and settled in Dublin. There she gave birth to their daughter, Robyn, in June 1999. But six weeks after the birth, the couple split and Lorraine returned to her hometown of Callan in Kilkenny. George remained in contact and, once every two weeks, visited Lorraine and the baby. He took a job in Limerick and was insistent his relationship with Lorraine would reignite. She, however, repeatedly told him that she didn't want to be with him: she had begun a new relationship.

A murderous rage started to boil within McGloin. On the day of the killing, 11 November 2001, he had travelled to Callan to look after his child. Lorraine suggested he take Robyn out, as it was a gloriously sunny day, rare for that time of year, but McGloin wanted to stay in the house.

Half an hour after he arrived Lorraine went to meet a friend in a bar where she worked part-time. During the afternoon McGloin phoned her and asked her if she was staying where she was. She told him she would. But McGloin rang back. This time he asked Lorraine to return to the house as he wanted to head back to Limerick. At her little girl's inquest, she reported: 'When I opened the front door that afternoon, Robyn jumped into my arms and George McGloin closed the door behind me. He had a frightening look on his face and his eyes were bulging.'

McGloin lashed out at Lorraine, punching her in the back and knocking her to the floor. She tried to defend herself but he jumped on top of her and continued to punch her. The little girl started to cry and McGloin grabbed a poker and pushed it into the child's stomach. In panic, Lorraine managed to drag him off their child and rushed to try to grab a knife to defend them. But he hit her on the back of the head with the poker. 'I kept screaming at him to leave Robyn alone,' Lorraine told the inquest. 'Then I saw blood on Robyn and splatters of blood on the wall.'

Somehow Lorraine managed to crawl out of the house to get help. Outside, Francis Laffan and his friend Martin McGuire saw her. She was hysterical and had a large wound at the back of her head but managed to tell them: 'He's killing my baby inside.' The men tried to get in through the front door of the house but it was locked, so they dashed around to the back.

In the living room they saw a man lying on the floor, holding a knife and bleeding from the stomach. They saw little Robyn on the couch beside him. Laffan told the inquest that the child was still alive. 'The man smiled up at me and spoke, but I did not know what he said.' Laffan worried that if he approached McGloin, the man might lash out at the child again. Eventually he went inside and lifted Robyn from the couch. He noticed a cut on her neck and realised she was dead.

In the meantime, locals had phoned gardaí. When Detective Frank McKenna and a colleague arrived, Robyn's body was outside on the pavement covered with a blanket. McGloin's was inside the house: he had stabbed himself five times in the heart and liver. An examination of Robyn's body would later show that she had suffered stab wounds to her heart and neck and had died from bleeding into her chest.

At the inquest, Lorraine said that a month before the attack, McGloin had become angry when she had told him she was seeing someone. Nothing else had signalled what was to come. The twenty-six-year-old mother had moved back to Callan so that her little girl could grow up surrounded by the family who loved her and where Lorraine herself had spent a happy childhood. McGloin had been working at the Midwestern Regional Hospital in Limerick and was within weeks of qualifying as an emergency medical technician.

While Stephen Byrne, Greg Fox and George McGloin were overcome by a murderous rage focused on their wife or partner, another father would stun those who knew and loved him, when he killed his little girl. Just a month before Stephen Byrne had stabbed Maeve and driven his little boys into the sea, a Dublin man buckled under the weight of his depression and strangled his five-year-old daughter because she refused to get dressed.

In 2002 James Byrne was found guilty while insane of the murder of little Nicole at Cromcastle Drive in Coolock on 6 July 2000. He had pleaded not guilty to murder, but admitted killing the child while suffering from depression by strangling her with his pyjama cord.

Byrne was described as a model parent, and Prosecution Counsel Patrick Gageby said in his opening speech that the case was far removed from most similar crimes, which usually involved dysfunctional families. James and his wife Sylvia worked, drank little and were devoted to their two children, Nicole and eleven-year-old James, he said. Before the killing, Byrne had been depressed and wasn't eating properly. The month before he strangled his little girl, the family had gone on holiday but he had forced them to return early. When they had got back, his wife was so worried about him that she had brought him to the family doctor, who prescribed medication for depression. At the same time, the court heard, Nicole's behaviour had become difficult and she had not wanted to go to school.

On the morning of the killing, Sylvia, who worked at the nearby Cadbury plant, left for work as usual at seven forty a.m. and her husband dropped James off at his tennis club. Nicole was in the car but had refused to get dressed and was still wearing her pyjamas. When they got home, he strangled the child and put her in his own bed. He had then tried to hang himself in the attic with a skipping rope but failed, so he drove to Dollymount where he tried to drown himself. He failed at that too, so he drove to Blessington Lakes and tried again to drown himself, once more without success.

When young James got back from his tennis club at lunchtime, he discovered his sister's body and went to a neighbour for help. At work, Sylvia was told that there had been an accident in the house.

Mr Gageby told the jury that Nicole was killed because Byrne had decided he wanted to commit suicide and didn't want to leave his wife with two children.

In her evidence, Sylvia Byrne said she had been worried about her husband's health and her daughter's behaviour for some weeks before the killing. Her daughter had complained of feeling sad, and when she asked why, Nicole had said, 'I don't know, Ma. I love you and I love my dad and I love James, but something is making me sad.' After his arrest, Sylvia had spoken to her husband at Sandymount Garda Station, where he told her: 'I killed her, Sylvia.' She told the court she was standing by her husband and that her family had been punished enough. Turning to the jury, she said Nicole's death would never leave her but, 'Jim loved her, too.'

State Psychiatrist Dr Charles Smith told the court that Byrne had been suffering from a serious depression before, during and after the killing. He had no doubt that the killing had been 'illness-driven'. However, he added, Byrne's illness was not psychotic in nature: serious depression carries with it a high risk of suicide, and while the sufferer does not normally bring someone with him, it may occur.

Seventeen-month-old Jack Brennan was killed by a mentally disturbed uncle in March 2000, just four months before Nicole was strangled by her depressed father. He was thrown into a quarry pond, where he was later discovered with a rope tied round his neck and a brick strung to his feet: he had been strangled. David Brennan was only eighteen when he choked his nephew to death. At his trial he was found guilty while insane, and was detained indefinitely in the Central Mental Hospital.

During his trial the Central Criminal Court heard medical evidence that David Brennan had been diagnosed as suffering from paranoid schizophrenia and often had delusional hallucinations while in a psychotic state.

Dr Charles Smith said Brennan had been in this confused state when he had killed the child. Brennan had told him that he killed baby Jack 'to relieve his sister from a bad future in relation to the child'. Brennan's mother, Patricia, said she had taken her son to Ardee Psychiatric Hospital on the night of the killing. He was prescribed medication but allowed home.

Shortly after the verdict, Paul Moore, solicitor, issued a brief statement on behalf of David Brennan's family: 'The past two years have been a most harrowing and difficult time for the family. They are relieved that there is now some closure. Nothing will bring Jack back. However, the family takes some comfort in the knowledge that David is at last receiving, and will continue to receive, the medical treatment which sufferers of his condition so require.'

Brennan's psychosis was caused by a chemical imbalance in his brain and the signs had been there from his early teens. He was expelled twice from school for trouble-making and drug-taking. His mother had had to bar him from the family home months before the murder of her grandson. During the four months he was out of her house, he had slept rough, and she eventually allowed him return. On the day of the murder, his GP had referred him to hospital but he wasn't admitted. Nobody ever suspected he was a danger to baby Jack, and those connected with the case testified that he had loved the baby. His sister Barbara had been asleep when he took Jack from his bed, put him in his buggy and strangled him near the quarry pond.

2

THE PLAN

Adrian Dunne and The Monageer Tragedy

Fear and panic hit Marian O'Brien instantly, as she read the headline: 'Four Bodies Found in County Wexford Home'. On the television remote control, she hit 104 and waited for the teletext news to appear on the screen. The colour drained from her face and her heart pounded. It was a family – a couple and their two children – and they had been discovered that morning. All were dead. A garda inquiry was under way but it was understood that officers weren't looking for anyone else in connection with the deaths.

'Please, God, don't let it be them.' Frantically she searched her handbag for her mobile phone. Her hands shook as she dialled Ciara's number. She waited for a ring tone. But there was nothing. She dialled again – she needed to hear Ciara's voice and be reassured that all was well.

On the television, the teletext information had been updated. The tragedy had taken place in Monageer. 'Oh, my

God, it's them! I know it's them,' she told her friend, who tried to tell her that everything would be alright. It was four p.m. on Monday, 23 April 2007, and Marian O'Brien's world as she knew it was about to change for ever.

She rang Directory Enquiries and was put through to Ferns Garda Station, but the phone rang out. She called again, and this time asked for Enniscorthy Garda Station, where the phone was picked up. The garda who answered couldn't provide her with any more information as to the identity of who had died. 'I just want to know if it's my daughter,' she begged. The officer said she would try to find out and call her back.

Marian scanned the few teletext paragraphs again. Monageer: the town where Ciara was living with her husband Adrian and their two little girls, Léan, who was just about to turn five, and three-year-old Shania. She picked up the phone again and rang her husband's mobile.

P.J. O'Brien was at work when he answered the call to his wife. He knew the minute he answered that something was desperately wrong. Marian was hysterical and gasping as she told him about the news on teletext. She told him she had phoned the garda stations but they couldn't tell her anything. P.J. tried to reassure her – but he was worried. He told her to phone a family friend, a garda inspector stationed not too far away in Baltinglass, Wicklow. Perhaps he could help. 'I'm on the way,' he said, grabbing his car keys. 'I'm sure everything will be OK.'

The O'Briens were not given to unnecessary panic but they had had so many sleepless nights in recent months, worrying about Ciara and their little grandchildren. They knew too well that Adrian had an unhealthy degree of control over Ciara, and was obsessed with keeping her and the girls all to himself. Could he have harmed them?

Marian closed her eyes and saw the smiling faces of the little girls: Léan with her brown curls, and Shania with her soft blonde mane. They were sweet little things who, despite their sight problems, were happy, healthy children who loved to play and giggle. Their arrival had brought out the best in Ciara, but fatherhood had changed Adrian for the worse.

At twenty-six, Ciara was the O'Briens' second daughter in a family of four. She had always been what her mother described as 'vulnerable'. She had been born in Letterkenny in Donegal, but when she was just two, her father's work had taken the family to Dublin. They had lived there until she was six when P.J. was transferred to Sligo and the family moved back to their native Donegal, settling in the little village of Burt. Ciara was a beautiful, sweet-natured child, but she struggled at school and could never quite keep up with her peers. When she was in fifth class, she was assessed as a slow learner, but P.J. and Marian were determined that they would give her every opportunity in life. They sent her to a local special-needs school where she received one-to-one tuition, which suited her. In 1994 she went on to another special school at Belmont, in nearby Derry City, and spent four years there.

Ciara loved children and often said she wanted 'a football team' of her own. After school she first attended a Training and Developmental Institute in Lifford, in Donegal, and then did an FAS training course. When she won a place to study as a childcare assistant at Park House, in Stillorgan, she was delighted and so were her family. Finally she would have the opportunity to train in what she really loved doing. While Park House offered her some independence, it was also a safe environment where she could learn at her own pace.

In the summer of 2000, when Ciara was still only nineteen, she was introduced to another resident of Park House by a mutual friend. Adrian Dunne was the fifth child of a family of nine born to Mary and Hughie Dunne, a touring musician, and he had been reared in a rural local-authority house in County Wexford. His parents were visually impaired, as were several of his siblings. Adrian had been born with congenital cataracts. As an infant and a young child, he underwent operations on his eyes. At eight, he started to have epileptic-type seizures, and in his teens he developed glaucoma, which blinded him. He had attended a mainstream primary school in Wexford, but in 1991, when he was thirteen, he had been assessed by a clinical psychologist as functioning at the upper limits of mild mental handicap, with an IQ of 64. He was sent to Our Lady of Fatima Special School in Wexford, where he sat the Junior Certificate in two subjects.

Adrian's health problems were never far away. When he left school he did a number of skills courses, but at eighteen he developed pneumonia and ended up in hospital. In the years that followed he suffered from renal colic, a severe pain associated with kidney stones, and hydrocele, an accumulation of fluids around a testicle, which resulted in surgery. Despite his health, he had always harboured a desire to become a journalist, and when he got a place on a FAS media training course in Dublin, he moved to Park House.

From the moment he met Ciara, Adrian decided she was 'the One'. She was smaller than him, with long, straight brown hair and a pretty face, always smiling. He had a domineering personality and liked to have things his own way. His girlfriend was submissive and could be easily manipulated if she disagreed with him. He liked to be in control and she looked up to him, hanging on his every word.

When she brought him home to meet her family in Donegal, the O'Briens were welcoming, if a little concerned about Ciara's ability to conduct an adult relationship. They had always wanted the best and the most for their daughter, but they couldn't help worrying about whether she was mature enough to handle the ups and downs of love. They hoped against hope that she wouldn't be hurt.

About twelve months into the courtship, Ciara became pregnant and the O'Briens decided the best thing for their daughter was to be near home where she could receive the support she would need when she had her baby. Adrian moved with her, and the couple shared a flat in Letterkenny until a relative of Ciara allowed them to move into a house in Bridgend at a low rent. Léan was born in May 2002 and shortly after was diagnosed with congenital cataracts.

Ciara took to motherhood like a duck to water. When she was discharged from hospital, a note was made about her learning difficulties but added that she was 'coping well'. A few weeks later, Léan's cataracts were removed. The baby spent a considerable time in hospital, followed by check-ups in the months that followed. The prognosis was good, and Ciara and Adrian were told that the little girl was likely to have 70 per cent of her sight.

While Ciara loved her new role as a mother, Adrian seemed to take his new status as man of the house to an extreme. He constantly told Ciara what to do and how to do it – even when it came to the baby. She saw nothing wrong with this. Whenever her family tried to challenge Adrian about it, he was defensive and Ciara always took his side. The O'Briens tried to be encouraging and supportive and a family friend even provided Adrian and Ciara with money to go to Disneyland in Florida after the traumas they had experienced during their first six months as parents. While they were there, they completely overspent their budget, lavishing gifts on Léan, and had to ring

Ciara's parents when they couldn't pay their hotel bill.

Back at home, they received every social welfare allowance they were entitled to, but found it hard to stick to a budget and racked up a number of loans with credit unions and from family members. Adrian, whose family had been in touch with Social Services throughout his life, began to restrict their involvement with his daughter. He took control of contact with social workers and cancelled early-development examinations and assessments.

Meanwhile, those who saw Ciara felt she was finding it hard to grasp basic concepts like nappy changes. At their insistence, Social Services in Donegal eventually arranged, after a series of failed attempts, for their early-intervention team to see Léan in April 2003. The team included a physiotherapist, a paediatric registrar and a counsellor for special needs. Their report found she had 'gross developmental delay', and couldn't sit without support, although she was almost a year old. They devised a plan for Léan to undergo speech therapy, special exercises and occupational therapy.

The family cancelled their next appointment, then also a developmental examination and a hearing assessment. Social workers tried to visit on an almost daily basis throughout July, but couldn't get access to the house and were told by a doctor that Ciara was now pregnant with the couple's second child.

Tensions between Adrian and the O'Briens reached new heights and he convinced Ciara to move nearer to his family in Wexford, far away from Donegal. There, he promised her, they would have nobody interfering in their lives, and a much better environment in which to rear their growing family. She agreed, but worried about what her parents would say if she moved so far away. Adrian persuaded her not to tell them and the couple waited until Ciara's parents were on holidays to move.

When the O'Briens returned, they had no idea where the pair had gone. It took them weeks to make contact with Ciara again.

In Wexford Adrian and Ciara moved twice before Shania was born in November. As they liaised with a new set of developmental workers about Léan, a public health nurse who visited them noted that Adrian 'has a personality disorder'. Until an appointment in October, the family attended their scheduled sessions for Léan but then started to cancel them and even moved house without telling her doctors.

Shania too had inherited congenital cataracts and underwent surgery for both eyes shortly after she was born. In an interview recorded by a public health nurse after the birth, Ciara 'came across as soft, gently spoken, lovely mothering qualities, caring, and liked information and took it on board'. As time went on Shania was also recognised as a slow developer but Léan was coming on. By her second birthday she had been referred for speech and language therapy, but it was noted that she was bright and her hearing test was normal. Still, the family continued to miss appointments or when health workers called to their home, they were out. They regularly changed their phone numbers and missed outpatient appointments without notice. Forms were returned unsigned relating to records from Donegal.

In Wexford Adrian had also become more controlling and supervised any visits Ciara's family made to her. The O'Briens felt distinctly unwelcome and had to stay in hotels. Adrian thwarted their efforts to see their daughter and grandchildren. When Shania was eighteen months old, the family moved again and settled in Wexford town where they decided to marry. Originally they planned a large wedding and Ciara intended inviting her extended family and friends from Donegal.

But Adrian had other ideas. On New Year's Eve of 2005 he sprang a surprise on her. He woke her at six thirty a.m. and told her to get dressed in her best clothes. He had secretly booked a church and had told his family the day before that they were getting married. His mother was to be maid of honour and his father, best man. The O'Briens only discovered that the wedding had taken place when a friend heard a request playing for the newlyweds on local radio. They were devastated and deeply worried for their daughter. They had done nothing wrong but Adrian was trying to keep them out of Ciara's life.

When the couple bought a car and designated Ciara as the driver, even though she hadn't a full licence, they broadened their horizons: they made regular trips to the seaside and to the shops, and went to football or hurling matches together. But while the car gave them a sense of adventure, it didn't give Ciara any more freedom. She had become very overweight and decided to join a gym in Gorey. She went two or three times a week, but every time she did, Adrian and the two girls would sit outside in the car waiting for her.

The O'Briens were at a loss. Contact with Ciara was slowly ceasing, and mostly when they rang her mobile, Adrian would answer and make up an excuse as to why she couldn't talk. Often he was downright rude.

Just before their first wedding anniversary, Adrian and Ciara moved again to Bree, and less than a year later, in July 2006, they made their final move to Monageer. It was their seventh home since Léan's birth. Often Marian O'Brien would travel all the way from the Inishowen Peninsula, a round trip of almost five hundred miles, to have a door closed in her face. She was out of her mind with worry about her daughter and feared that Adrian would harm her. She often broke down in front of friends as she told them about the dreadful situation.

In November 2006 the O'Briens made their last visit to Wexford. They were not allowed see Ciara, and while they tried to continue to keep in contact with her by telephone and text message, they were rarely able to talk with her. When they began receiving aggressive texts from Ciara's phone, warning them to stay away from her and her children, they were sure Adrian was sending them. His actions worried them and they began to wonder what he was capable of. Marian tried to alert authorities in the area about her concerns. She called gardaí, social workers and a nurse, and said she was afraid he might harm the family. But while Adrian was isolating Ciara from her nearest and dearest, he was doing the same with the health authorities. At home he always answered the door and the telephone and did all the talking for them.

Now a family was dead in Wexford.

Marian waited by the phone, hoping that her inspector friend from Wicklow would find out quickly if the tragedy in the neighbouring county had anything to do with Ciara. Within ten minutes, her worst fears had been confirmed: he called back and broke the news that the family that had been found dead that morning were indeed Ciara, Adrian, Léan and Shania.

By the time he reached his wife, P.J. had also heard the news. The couple were inconsolable and suffering from shock. Surrounded by family and close friends, they awaited further news as they tried to comprehend what had happened.

At the same time, four hundred miles away in Wexford, Mary Dunne and her son Cornelius were arriving at 29 Moin Rua. The mother and son had been at a centre run by the National Council for the Blind an hour before when Mary had heard the news.

Mary was distraught. She was still reeling from burying her son James just weeks ago. He had committed suicide. He and Adrian had been very close and were both die-hard Wexford fans. Also, it was less than two weeks since she had attended a mass for the first anniversary of the death of her husband Hugh. Now she was dealing with the news that her fifth child was gone, and with him, Ciara and the girls. It was too much for any mother to have to bear.

Across Ireland, newsrooms buzzed with the breaking story from the small village near Enniscorthy, and details were fast emerging that Adrian, who had been blind, might have smothered his daughters, strangled his wife and then hanged himself. His body had been found in the hallway, while Ciara's and the girls' were in the sitting room.

Journalists were dispatched to the area and editors planned major coverage in the Tuesday's papers. By Monday evening, stories were being filed that suggested the Health Service Executive and the gardaí had discussed the family over the weekend. It also transpired that the family had paid a macabre visit to a funeral director's in the town on the previous Friday. Concerned, the undertaker had contacted a priest, Father Richard Redmond, who was based at nearby New Ross. He had known the Dunnes well before they moved to Monageer. He confirmed to the media that he had indeed visited the family on Friday night and spent two hours with them.

Adrian's brother, Sebastian, was interviewed and told of how the couple were planning a move to Liverpool to start a new life. He said they had told him they were trying for another child and he suspected that Ciara was pregnant. The Dunnes were adamant from the outset that Adrian could not have acted alone: 'He was blind. How can a blind guy kill three people?' Sebastian told reporters.

Almost immediately there were calls for an inquiry into the tragedy and for the HSE to explain its inaction over that fateful weekend. Monageer was an unknown backwater, but in late April 2007 Adrian Dunne had made sure it was firmly etched into the conscience of a nation.

The initial focus of the garda investigation was fixed on the New Ross undertakers, and a bizarre phone call they had taken twenty days previously. It had kicked off a countdown to the haunting deaths of an entire family. At Cooney's funeral home in the heart of Wexford town, 4 April had started like any other day. Arrangements were being made for funerals and paperwork was being signed off. The small family firm was open for business as usual.

Cooney's has long been a fixture of New Ross and is well-regarded for its commitment to the people of the little town over three generations. The Cooneys themselves are highly respected locally, known for their sympathetic and professional manner in dealing with the bereaved.

Over the decades the Cooneys have seen it all when it comes to the business of death, and have many a story to tell of the odd items people have wanted buried with them, of the clothes they wished to be laid out in and of the music they wanted played at the service. None of this had been as odd as the phone call a staff member took that morning, when a man, who refused to identify himself, asked a series of pointed questions about his own funeral. The call wasn't totally out of the ordinary: many people pre-arrange their funeral so that they are not a burden in death to anyone else. The man said he had just buried his brother, a suicide, and that his father had died the previous year. A second brother had been killed in a car accident twelve months ago, he said. He himself was married with a couple of children and wanted to make his own funeral arrangements. The staff member sympathised with him over the recent tragedies and assured him that funeral arrangements could be made in advance. Then he enquired gently as to what the man had in mind.

He asked if he could be buried in his own family grave and whether it was possible to get white coffins for adults. He was told that white coffins were available, at special request, for adults. As for the family grave, that was a matter for the owner. In the background, the funeral director's staff member could make out the voice of a woman, who seemed to be prompting the caller. As the whispers at the other end of the line became more audible, the man eventually said that his wife was anxious to know if a child could be buried with each parent.

Taken aback by such a strange question, the staff member explained that if a family was unfortunate enough to lose their lives in a multiple tragedy, their remains would usually be laid to rest in their own plot, rather than a family grave, but she assured him that it was indeed possible for a child to be buried with each parent. The man appeared satisfied. He then told her he was going to make a will and asked her what an 'executor' was. She told him it was someone nominated to carry out the tasks or wishes in the will.

He moved on to his next question: 'Can a will be contested?' He added that he was blind and that his mother-in-law would take the children from him if his wife died. 'This is my greatest fear,' he confided, and told the staff member that his mother-in-law didn't like him.

As she put down the phone, the staff member felt uneasy. The call had been extremely odd, and while her daily work kept her mind on other things, the conversation with the mystery man kept popping back into her mind. A few days later, she told Joanne Cooney, the funeral director, about it.

Two weeks later the phone rang and Joanne Cooney picked it up. 'Cooney Undertakers, how may I help you?' she asked.

The male caller failed to identify himself but immediately launched into questions about whether or not he could have an adult white coffin if he died. Joanne was surprised but assured him that, yes, he could. 'And can my wife have a white coffin too?' he asked.

'Yes,' said Joanne, and remembered the call her staff member had taken.

'OK, good,' said the caller, and went on to ask about making pre-planned funeral arrangements for his children.

Joanne could barely disguise her shock but she wanted to keep the man on the line and try to find out who he was, so she behaved normally. She briefed him on the Golden Charter Funeral Plan, a UK-based company with a representative in Ireland – she knew the woman fairly well, from having had dealings with her and from the odd bit of business she had put her way when an elderly person with no family wanted to arrange their funeral before they died. She told the caller that the company would devise a 'plan' for those who wanted to arrange their funerals while they were still alive rather than leave it up to loved ones.

That seemed to grab his attention. The caller asked Joanne a number of specific questions, which she was unable to answer. Among his concerns were the deaths of his two children who, he insisted, had to be included in his plan. She asked his name several times over the course of the conversation but he told her that she did not need to know it at that stage. Having got nowhere with him, she suggested he should ring the representative himself and put the questions to her directly. She would furnish him with the number.

But he hadn't quite finished: he asked about a grave, and

told her that his family had a plot that already contained the bodies of his father and his two brothers. He asked could his wife be buried in that grave, and Joanne told him she could if he had written permission from his mother. He told her it was a six-plot grave and calculated that with three bodies already in it, plus another two, there would still be room for his mother.

Joanne found the conversation deeply disturbing. She had a gut feeling that this was no prank call and that the man, whoever he was, might have a plan already for his family. After hanging up, she rang Mary, the Golden Charter representative, and alerted her to the likelihood that the unidentified male might call. She briefed her on the nature of the conversation that had caused her concern and urged her to try to get his name and address, if and when he phoned.

It was rare for Golden Charter to deal directly with clients. Usually the plan would be agreed with a funeral director who would approach them on their client's behalf to set up payments for the service. Joanne wished Mary well and they wondered would either of them hear from the caller again.

Minutes later Mary's mobile rang again, and a male caller identified himself as 'Adrian'. She scribbled down the name. He explained that he had been given her number by the funeral director at Cooney's Undertakers in New Ross. He wanted to know all about her company and what the plan entailed. Mary asked Adrian where he was from and, despite his strong Wexford accent, thought he said he was from 'Mullinavat near Ferns'. She couldn't be sure but she wrote the names down on her notepad.

Trying to engage him further in conversation about his home town, Mary told him that there were funeral directors much closer to him than New Ross and offered to suggest some. But he was adamant that his local priest had recommended the Cooneys.

Then the questions started.

'Can I be buried in a Liverpool jersey?'

'Can we have adult-size white coffins?'

'Can the children be buried in their favourite clothes and Liverpool jerseys?'

'Can a child be buried with each of the parents?'

Mary drew a breath and gently tried to explain that, in the normal course of events, children would outlive their parents so he should not be worried about such matters as whether or not they could be buried with them and what they would wear in the coffin. He listened but was quick with a response. He told her that friends of his had been on holiday the year before in Spain and that they had all been killed in a car accident. 'Do I need to go to a solicitor to make sure that arrangements are carried out in accordance with my wishes?' he asked.

Mary told him that that wouldn't be necessary. He could nominate someone to be provided with a copy of the plan.

'Well, what about a priest?' he asked.

'Absolutely, that's no problem – and if the priest is transferred to another parish over the course of time, the instructions can be left in the parochial house,' Mary told him.

Happy with her response, Adrian asked what the next step should be. She told him to go back to Joanne Cooney and talk to her. Again, he asked about family graves and wanted to know how much his plan would cost. Again, Mary told him to talk to Joanne. 'OK, but what if something happened and I hadn't paid in full?' he asked.

Eventually he thanked her and assured her he would be ringing Joanne to proceed.

Baffled, Mary hit the call log button on her mobile and dialled Joanne's number. She told her everything about the conversation she had just had with Adrian. Joanne knew she was right to have been concerned from the beginning. She had a mobile number for a garda acquaintance and decided to phone him for his advice. 'I'm just very concerned,' she said, and detailed the bits of information she had garnered about her caller's possible identity, then briefed him on the man's obsession with his children's burial. She didn't have his full name but she knew that a brother had recently committed suicide. She would later say: 'I just had a bad feeling.'

The garda told her that if anything else came to her or if Adrian rang again, she should contact him.

The following morning Joanne's mother was manning the phones at Cooney's, when a man rang, said his name was Adrian Dunne, from Monageer, and made an appointment to see Joanne the following day at two o'clock.

Throughout the day Joanne pondered on the meeting. One way or another, she surmised, she had to get some photographic evidence of this man. The business had a flower shop attached to it with a CCTV system and she decided to have him brought through it to her office, so she would capture him on film.

At ten past two, the following day, Adrian, Ciara, Léan and Shania arrived at the funeral home. Joanne took the four into her office and sat them down, trying to act as normally as she could, despite her rising anxieties.

As they settled in, she extended her hand to Adrian and introduced herself. 'So, I'm Joanne. We spoke on the phone. Now, how can I help you?' she asked politely.

Adrian immediately took charge of the conversation and said he wanted to make his funeral arrangements. He told Joanne he wanted a solid oak coffin in white and he wanted to be dressed in a Liverpool football jersey, jeans and socks when he was laid out. 'Where do you want to be waked? In a hospital or a funeral home, for example?' she asked him.

He turned to Ciara and asked her what she thought. For a moment she considered it, then decided, one night in a funeral home with the coffins closed. She nodded and smiled, evidently satisfied with her decision.

'Can the children be put into the same coffins as us?' he asked. Joanne looked at the two little girls playing happily on the floor beside their parents. They were immaculately dressed. She looked back at Adrian. 'Well, they can,' she said slowly, 'but only if they are under six years of age at the time of death.' She waited for his reaction but he was very focused on the job at hand.

He told her that they wanted the Liverpool anthem, 'You'll Never Walk Alone' to be sung and the Guns N' Roses version of Led Zeppelin's classic 'Stairway To Heaven' to be played at the funeral mass. Again he asked about the possibility of being buried in his family plot, and for the second time Joanne told him he would need the written permission of his mother. But he said he didn't want his mother to know about it. He turned to Ciara and asked her if she thought they should get their own plot. As the girls played at her feet, Ciara said they should, but only the four of them were ever to be buried in it. Next, they detailed exactly what they wanted to mark their passing: heart-shaped black headstones. They would be committed to the grave after the Clonroche curate, Father Richard Redmond, had said the funeral mass.

Joanne turned to Ciara. 'And what are your wishes?' she asked her.

Ciara smiled. 'The same as Adrian described,' she said, looking at him lovingly.

'And what about arrangements for the children?' Joanne asked.

'Well, we want Léan to be buried with Adrian and Shania to be buried with me,' she told her matter-of-factly. 'They are to be dressed in their "Dora" jeans and tops . . . Oh, and the jeans are at home in the house.'

Joanne could hardly believe what she was hearing. She looked long and hard at the young couple in front of her and slowly told them that she was sure the children would grow up, get married and have their own children.

Ciara interrupted: 'That will never happen,' she said. She added that if they did die after the age of six, they were to be buried in their own white coffins.

Joanne asked her who would look after the children, should she die before them. Ciara told her that a friend from Limerick had been named in the will as their guardian.

The discussion turned to money and the Golden Charter Plan, which, Joanne explained, they could pay in instalments over a twelve-month period or in full. They were troubled by the amount but Ciara mentioned that they had a Canada Life insurance policy, which Joanne told them would fund their funerals.

Joanne shifted in her seat, cleared her throat and asked the Dunnes if they intended giving a copy of the completed Plan to their respective families. Surely they'll be alarmed if they see the details in it, she thought. But Adrian and Ciara said they had no intention of doing that. Adrian again took charge, and said that Father Redmond was a personal family friend and that he would be in charge of the funerals when they died.

Over the course of the meeting Ciara spoke about car accidents and suicide, and Adrian claimed that many single-vehicle accidents were suicide. Ciara mentioned that friends of theirs, a family of six, had been killed in a car crash in Spain.

The meeting lasted forty-five minutes, and throughout, the

Dunnes were calm and relaxed while the children appeared happy and healthy. They played and laughed as their parents, slowly and insistently, listed their funeral wishes. Towards the end, Joanne went back over the list of instructions to make sure that the couple were aware of the macabre shopping list they had drawn up.

'"If all four of us die together we are to be interred in the new double grave in Boolavogue and no one else is ever to be buried there. We require a black marble headstone and kerbing. The headstone is to be in the shape of a heart, there is to be a Liverpool crest on it, with red and white stones – Liverpool colours,"' she read.

'You want two white coffins, with Adrian buried in a Liverpool jersey, jeans and socks. The children are to be buried, one with each parent. They are to wear "Dora" jeans, which are in your house, and Liverpool jerseys. And you want the listed music played at the funeral?' she asked them. Both nodded.

'What really kept fazing me through the whole thing was the kids – they were adamant on getting the wishes of the kids through. Something kept telling me that it was going to happen soon,' she said later.

Before they left, they agreed to return on Monday to sign the plan. Although Joanne was uneasy, she hoped that their commitment to return had bought some time.

She wasn't to know that Adrian Dunne's plans were firmly in place.

The previous February Adrian had started making enquiries about moving his family to Liverpool and had made contact with an Irish Community Centre there to ask about schools for the blind, housing, welfare payments and work. Towards the end of March he had even phoned an estate agent about buying a home, saying he could pay up to £300,000 even though he already had debts of more than thirty thousand euro that he couldn't pay. By April he had ceased contact with the Liverpool authorities and changed his plan for his family.

The day after his first anonymous phone call to Joanne's colleague, the family had arrived at a solicitor's office in Enniscorthy to make their wills, which were simple. Either spouse would inherit everything if the other died, and if both died, the children would receive their estate. Dunne had nominated Father Redmond, his brother Sebastian and a friend from Limerick to be executors of both wills and the female friend was also appointed guardian of the children. During the meeting the little girls sat in their parents' laps and sang 'You'll Never Walk Alone'.

An appointment to sign the wills was cancelled shortly before the final meeting with the undertaker.

Adrian had also made enquiries about a lapsed insurance policy and arranged a meeting with the insurer, but had cancelled it. Four weeks prior to the tragedy, the couple had visited a Euro Discount Store in Wexford, where Ciara had asked for a Liverpool teddy or any other memorabilia of the football team. She told the shop assistant she was looking for something to put in a child's coffin. A week after James's suicide, Adrian, Ciara and the girls visited another shop in New Ross and ordered two Dora dolls.

As she watched the family leave her premises, Joanne picked up her mobile and again called her garda contact. She told him that the man to whom she had earlier alerted him had arrived at her office with his wife and children. As she recounted the meeting with the Dunnes she could hardly believe what she was saying. She hoped the information she had garnered would be useful. If she was right with her suspicions, the family needed help. She read out the couple's full names, address and dates of birth and told the officer everything she had learnt about Adrian's brother's death. Then she described the plan and the instructions to be carried out in the event of the family's deaths. The Dunnes had told her that they had made wills: the solicitors were Enniscorthy-based James and Hugh Dunne. She added that the Dunnes had given her permission to provide Father Redmond with a copy of the plan. The conversation was short and her contact asked her to drop a copy of the Dunnes' instructions into the garda station when she had typed them up. He told her to contact Father Redmond to make him aware of the arrangements.

As she hung up, she hoped she had put them off doing anything to harm themselves or their children that day, in telling them that she wouldn't have the plan ready for signing until after the weekend.

She could not have guessed that such officialdom was exactly the type of thing that Adrian Dunne had ignored throughout his life, and particularly when it came to paperwork. As far as he was concerned, he had made his arrangements.

Joanne rang Father Redmond but had to leave a message for him. At five thirty that evening he called back, and for the second time that day, she recounted the funeral arrangements the Dunne family had made with her just hours before. 'I believe you have agreed to be an executor of the wills?' she asked him.

But the priest assured her that he hadn't and neither had he referred Adrian Dunne to Cooney's. There was a long silence. Then Joanne asked the priest what he thought they should do. He said he would phone the garda and visit the Dunne home that night.

Father Redmond knew Adrian and Ciara Dunne, and periodically received phone calls from Adrian to discuss his eye problems and, more recently, his brother's suicide. He was sure that Adrian had been traumatised by James's death: Adrian had telephoned him only recently to say that he was listening to an American television programme and had heard that those who killed themselves went to hell. Adrian appeared to be a nice young man. Father Redmond had known his mother and late father since 2000, when he had begun working as a priest in Clonroche. They were a large family but seemed close-knit. He knew that Ciara and Adrian had lived in Donegal before moving to Wexford.

He would usually spend Friday evening watching television or preparing a sermon for Sunday mass, but that night he grabbed his car keys and set out on the eighteen-mile journey to Monageer. In the car he phoned Adrian and told him he would be in the area and wanted to drop in. The young man told him he was visiting the family grave in Boolavogue but would meet him back at the house.

It would later emerge that he had brought Ciara and the girls to view burial plots after their meeting with Joanne Cooney.

Arriving in Monageer shortly before seven o'clock, Father Redmond decided to call to the presbytery to see if the local parish priest, Father Bill Cosgrave, would accompany him, but he was out.

As soon as he got to the door Adrian answered it, with Léan and Shania at his feet, smiling and shy but excited by their visitor. The girls were neatly dressed, with their hair in little ponytails. Making small talk about the weather, Adrian led the priest to the sitting room where they continued to chat until Ciara emerged from the kitchen, walked straight over to

Adrian and perched herself on his knee. After about half an hour, the curate decided he was going to have to bring up the awkward reason for his out-of-the-blue visit. He told the couple gently that he was concerned about information that had been passed on to him from their earlier visit to the funeral home, the complicated arrangements they had made for their burial, which included their young children. He told them he hoped they weren't going to do anything to themselves or their children.

Ciara was indignant and irate. 'What are you suggesting?' she asked, flabbergasted. 'Do you think we're going to hurt our children or harm ourselves? I wouldn't allow anyone to harm my children.'

Adrian touched her leg and leaned forward. Slowly he explained to the priest that, as he was blind and Ciara did the driving, it was important that their affairs were in order, should anything happen to them. 'Have you signed off on your own will?' he asked him.

Father Redmond decided to change the subject and asked the couple how their own families were keeping. Adrian answered that they were estranged from their extended families and that Ciara had been very badly treated by hers. He said he and Ciara liked to keep to themselves as they didn't relate to their neighbours and the children on the street were rough with their girls so they couldn't allow them out to play. Ciara nodded in agreement. Adrian then said that he was hoping to move to Liverpool, where they were planning to make a new life for themselves away from the isolation they were suffering.

Ciara offered to make some tea and asked the priest if he would like to take a look around their house while they waited for the kettle to boil. The kitchen was sparse. There was no oven, no table and no chairs. A pressure cooker stood on a worktop and Ciara told him they used it to make food. The girls' room was painted pink and two fabric Barbie wardrobes stood in a corner.

As she brought him back to the sitting room, Ciara asked Father Redmond if he would be paid for coming to see them that evening. It was an unusual question but appeared to be asked in innocence, so he assured her that it was simply part of his ministry to visit. Ciara resumed her position on her husband's knee and told her visitor that she and Adrian were not planning to have any more children because of the eye problems.

Throughout the priest's visit, Adrian sent and received texts. During the subsequent inquiry it would emerge that he was in conversation with the 'friend' from Limerick whom he and Ciara had named in their wills as the future guardian of their children. She had had no idea she was so dear to Adrian that she could be considered in such a role. In fact, recently she had felt pretty much used and abused by Adrian and Ciara.

She had first met the Dunnes in 2005 and they had developed a close relationship, or so she had thought. A year later Adrian had asked her if he could have details of her laser card, as he was having problems paying his Sky Television account and had no such card himself. When she received her bank statement she quickly realised that instead of the seventy-five euro he had asked her for, he had made a number of withdrawals totalling a staggering €1,669.

Angry, she had phoned Adrian – but he had blamed Sky for a mix-up and promised to pay her back. The money was never forthcoming. Months later she had received a text from Adrian asking her to phone him immediately. He told her that his brother James had committed suicide. Later that day he had rung her again to say that another brother had been killed in a traffic accident. A few days later he had texted her to tell her that his mother had had a stroke and she, too, had died. As with the others involved in his intricate plan, he had made an arrangement to meet her but cancelled. On the day he went into Joanne Cooney's office, he had said he wanted to pay her back but texted her to say he had forgotten an appointment with a solicitor in Cork for the reading of James's will. As Father Redmond sipped tea in his house Adrian was arranging to meet her the following day.

After two hours the priest got up to leave. Ciara and Adrian accompanied him to the door. The girls were sitting on a wall outside, watching other children play on the road. The family's blue Nissan Micra was in the drive. Father Redmond got into his car, waving to the girls as he drove off.

He hadn't been long home when he received a call from Adrian, at ten thirty, checking that he had made it back safely. He could hear the children playing in the background. He told Adrian he would be in touch and would be back to visit shortly. He felt a bit more relaxed, having seen the family but he still wasn't happy about them as he retired to bed.

Given the tragedy that was about to unfold, it now seems likely that Adrian had phoned late that evening to reassure himself that the priest had gone home, and not to the authorities, after leaving the house.

The following morning Father Redmond tried to phone Father Cosgrave to tell him of the happenings of the day before, but there was no reply. He tried Adrian's number but the call was immediately diverted to message.

In the meantime Joanne's garda contact had arrived for duty at the station at midday. He found that Joanne had delivered the typed funeral arrangements by hand the previous evening. As he read them, the detail, especially about the children, shocked him and he decided to contact his superintendent as a matter of urgency. His boss was off duty for the day and it was an unprecedented call, but he felt he had to make it.

The superintendent told him he would ring his colleague, Superintendent Peter Finn, who had responsibility for the Monageer area and brief him on the situation.

The garda phoned Father Redmond and told him that Superintendent Finn would be in touch with him.

Over the course of the next few hours Superintendent Finn contacted both Father Redmond and the local child care manager who relayed information to him from a social worker that there was no file on the family, which meant the children were not 'at risk'.

Finn made further enquiries about the family through a local garda sergeant, who knew little about them, although officers had made a few calls to the house after reports of nuisance behaviour by neighbours' children. It was a tough one. Was Joanne's document a suicide note or a reasonable set of instructions drawn up by a cautious family? It was decided to send a patrol car to the estate to keep an eye on the house. At twelve thirty a.m. the officers saw that the lights in the house were off, the car was parked in the drive and everything appeared normal.

The following morning Father Cosgrave touched base with Father Redmond and made his way out to the house at 29 Moin Rua. He knocked on the door but there was no reply. The car was in the drive and the blinds were down. Over the next forty-eight hours social health care workers spoke to each other on the phone, but it wasn't until Monday morning that it was decided social workers would visit the family.

Nobody had seen or heard from the Dunnes since Father

Redmond's visit on Friday night. By Monday morning Father Cosgrave, too, had called again. He rang the bell at 29 Moin Rua shortly after eleven a.m. but no one answered. The car hadn't moved and the blinds were still down. Then he spotted containers of milk on the doorstep. He went straight home and rang Father Redmond. The priest called Joanne and told her about his visit on Friday and how he had failed to make contact since. 'Go and check the house. I'm telling you there's something wrong,' she advised him.

Shortly before lunch Father Redmond phoned Superintendent Finn and said he was very worried. A second patrol car was sent out to the house. The two officers who arrived knocked on the front door and then at the back, but there was no reply. They saw the milk on the doorstep and realised that the car hadn't moved all weekend. The blinds were drawn. One bent down and looked through the letterbox. Squinting into the darkness inside, he made out what looked like a man hanging. He called his colleague and together they went to the back and kicked in the door.

In the hallway they found Adrian. He was suspended from an open attic hatch with a strap around his neck. His toes were just inches from the floor and an upended box lay near his feet. He was dressed in a Glasgow Celtic jersey and a pair of jeans. In the living room the officers discovered Ciara on the floor. There was a ligature around her neck. She was wearing a brown jumper and blue jeans. Léan and Shania were seated at either end of the sofa, toe to toe. They might have been asleep. A pillow was perched on top of the sofa back between them. They were dressed in pyjamas and each had a Dora the Explorer doll tucked under her arm.

The officers called into base and briefed Superintendent Finn on their findings. They secured the scene while others summoned the assistance of the Garda Technical Bureau and the State Pathologist. The Garda Press Office was also notified, unusually early for a tragedy. As the crime-scene tape went up, two social workers arrived to visit the family. Soon a local GP arrived, and declared all four dead.

Ten minutes after Marian O'Brien had read the shocking news on teletext, Father Redmond and Father Cosgrave were giving her daughter, her grandchildren and Adrian Dunne the last rites.

As the media descended on the estate, Adrian's mother and brother arrived. By seven p.m. the house was swamped with a team from the ballistics, fingerprints, photography and mapping sections of the Technical Bureau. As evening fell, the Deputy State Pathologist examined the four bodies before they were removed to the mortuary at Wexford General Hospital.

The following day Sebastian Dunne identified his brother, his sister-in-law and their two children before the postmortems got under way. Tests showed that Adrian had died from hanging, but there was no indication of assault or restraint. A low level of alcohol was present in his blood but no drugs. Ciara had been strangled but bruising under her hair suggested she had been struck with a blunt instrument. She also had a black eye. The pathologist concluded that the injuries were enough to render her unconscious. He told the police that it was highly likely that the ligature was placed around her neck while she was unconscious as there was no evidence to suggest she had struggled to free it. In particular, he noted that her fingernails were neatly manicured and intact. Léan and Shania had been smothered. The elder, Léan, showed no evidence of injury but the pathologist was able to establish that Shania had been face down for several hours after death before being turned onto her back. She had two minor bruises on her scalp but no other evidence of trauma.

A pink Nokia mobile phone was found in the attic and a silver one in the hallway. The SIM cards, which lay close by, had been removed and broken in half across the copper interface, rendering them useless to analysts. Experts established that the pink one had Ciara's fingerprints while the silver model had been used by Adrian. The forensic scientist who examined them immediately recognised that whoever had done it was forensically aware and had cut them to destroy data stored on them. All that remained on the handsets was a number of sexually explicit texts between Adrian and Ciara's phones.

And also one text, written by Adrian, to a local radio journalist's mobile phone:

> Pleas ring father r from Wexford and tell him Ciara and Adrian are so very sorry. We nott going to Livepol. Instad we pick heaven … Please for give.

He had hit the digits 058 instead of 085 at the start of the number and it had never been received. It had been written on the Saturday morning, 21 April at ten seventeen a.m. – just an hour before Father Cosgrave first called to the house.

At nine twenty-seven that morning, investigators were able to ascertain that a call had been made to a chat line. Four minutes later, the credit balance on the phone was checked. An inquiry team would later consider all of the evidence and conclude that by the time the suicide text was sent, Ciara and the girls were dead.

Within days of the tragedy, and as gardaí continued their investigations, the Dunne family were quick to defend Adrian. Initially they stated that, as he was blind, he couldn't have acted alone and insisted that he and Ciara had together hatched a suicide pact. Mary Dunne then said that Adrian couldn't have orchestrated the deaths: she believed Ciara had killed her daughters.

Ciara's parents had maintained a dignified silence in Donegal as they attempted to plan their daughter's funeral. They were adamant that they would bring her and the children home and bury them together in Burt, Donegal, in the little graveyard located close to the O'Brien family home. They were never going to allow Adrian Dunne to have his final wishes and would go to court if need be to ensure that his plan was not carried out.

As they negotiated with the Dunne family over the burials, they requested that local TD Jim McDaid give a brief interview to try to clear Ciara's name. 'Ciara was a very impressionable young woman. He was a very dominant figure,' he told a local radio station. 'Her parents were up and down to Wexford on a number of occasions because of their concerns for their daughter's safety . . . I know her mother Marian was devastated at times and very distraught and would break down in front of friends. Every time they went to Wexford, they were fobbed off. Every time they were told to go away. Ciara had to obey his orders.' He conceded that Adrian was a loving father to his children but said, 'Like all domineering people, he tended to isolate his family.'

Less than a week after she had visited the funeral home to plan her own burial, Ciara Dunne began her last journey home accompanied by her two little daughters. As part of the agreement they had been waked in the Dunne family home and then the bodies were released to the O'Briens.

As Ciara and her girls were buried at St Aengus Church, Adrian was already beneath the ground three hundred miles away at Boolavogue Cemetery in Wexford. His family had ensured that some of his wishes were fulfilled, but in Donegal the funeral comprised traditional hymns and readings, with white roses and lilies covering the three coffins.

Afterwards Dr McDaid said that he could not describe the heartache that the deaths had brought to the O'Brien family: 'I have seen children die during my work but I have never seen two children murdered – or three children, because Ciara was only a child too.'

The 154-page report of the Monageer Inquiry that followed was published in May 2009. It was heavily censored to protect the identity of individuals who had figured in the investigation. It did, however, mention that the family had mounting debts and had run up more than three thousand euro in phone bills and that Adrian was an avid chat-line user. It stated that even if the gardaí or Social Services had called to the Dunne home during the weekend they had died, it was unlikely the tragedy could have been averted, given the couple's capacity to provide a plausible explanation for their bizarre funeral plans. It named Adrian as the driving force behind the planning and execution of the deaths. It failed to find a single, definitive motive behind them, but it called for the provision of a national out-of-hours social work service to ensure an appropriate response to serious child protection and welfare concerns. It also recommended greater training for frontline staff, a review of management structures in the HSE and better mechanisms for the early identification of children at risk.

During the inquest, the coroner for North Wexford, Dr Sean Nixon, said that both parents may have planned the deaths for a little while. 'They loved their children, there was no doubt about that. Familicide is like that: the Dunne family was quite united and the children were loved – they were not disliked or anything. They and their well-being were always central to Ciara and Adrian's life. The children's lives were taken under the misguided belief that there was a better life somewhere else.'

Many disagree, particularly those who knew and loved Ciara. They believe that, in her childlike innocence, she thought she was bringing her children to Liverpool, possibly to see a football match, and that the plans she had made with Adrian were no more than a precaution lest they all died together on their journey.

3

YOU WILL NEVER SEE HER FACE AGAIN
The Deirdre Crowley Tragedy

Summer 1999, Portlaoise
The woman in the shopping-centre car park looked around anxiously. She hadn't seen him for twelve years but the feelings were as strong as ever. She scanned the cars for his face – his beautiful face. And then she saw him. He was a bit older now but as handsome as she remembered. She wanted to talk to him, but he looked as if he had other things on his mind. He pulled up beside her in his red Toyota Starlet and told her to get in. He was anxious, sweating a bit. He needed her now more than ever and, just as they had promised one another all those years before, she would be there for him – no matter what. He told her about the child and the little girl's strange, depressed mother. He told her he was scared he was going to lose his child forever. He told her his plan and he begged her to help. Of course she'd help. She'd do anything for him. Anything.

* * *

Devastated mother Christine O'Sullivan thanked the journalist and wondered would the interview she had just given, by some miracle, prompt someone this time to pick up the phone and end her torture. Her ex-partner Chris Crowley had abducted their daughter, Deirdre, more than twenty months ago, and they had not been seen since. Surely someone knew where they were. Surely Chris would recognise her pain if he happened to read this article in the *Sunday People*. It was for the UK edition of the tabloid and would be printed that weekend, 26 August 2001. Even if Chris intended to continue torturing her, she hoped someone might recognise them from the pictures she had lent the paper and maybe something would come of it.

The journalist was a nice guy called Frank Peters, an affable man who had interviewed her with great sensitivity. He had promised her he would make sure the website she had set up – www.deirdrecrowley.com – was mentioned: anyone with information could find numbers there to call. She knew a lot of journalists, these days, particularly the locals, Barry Roche and Ann Mooney, both based in her native Cork. They rang her regularly for updates on her situation. Others came to see her sporadically, to do articles around Deirdre's birthday and at Christmas.

It was always hard to talk about it but she had chosen her words carefully to reassure Chris and try to appeal to whatever they had once shared. She had told Frank about the day in December 1999 that Deirdre had been taken out of her life. She had been just four-and-a-half, and Christine was dreading seeing another birthday pass, Deirdre's sixth, without any word of her. She told him she worried every day for how the little girl was coping without her, probably believing that her mother had abandoned her. This time Christine had appealed directly to Chris, telling him she had no interest in pressing charges or seeing him punished in any way. 'I just want her back safe and well. If you love Deirdre as much as you say you do, then you will do this for her,' she had said.

Christine sighed and poured herself a cup of tea. 'How do you cope?' Peters had asked her. How did she? She closed her eyes and pictured Deirdre dressing her little dolls, trailing around the house behind her in a pair of high heels she had 'borrowed' from the back of Christine's wardrobe, lipstick daubed across her face, shining bright blue eyes and a smile that would break your heart. But where was she? Christine thought of a beach in the South of France where a little girl, tanned and happy, was playing in the sand. She wondered had she lost her baby teeth, what size her feet were now and was her hair still in a neat little bob, or long and hanging over her shoulders.

Not a minute had passed over the previous twenty months when she hadn't thought of Deirdre. She was in her mind first thing in the morning and last thing at night. She even dreamed about her. Doing an interview always wore her out but it was important she kept it up. Some day Deirdre would see her on a television show or in a newspaper and would know that she had never given up the fight to find her.

She thought now about that morning and tried to remember every detail of her little angel's face, her roguish grin, her blonde hair tucked neatly behind her ears. She could still see her skipping down the drive towards her father's car, turning to wave kisses to her and then calling, 'Bye, Mum.' For some reason Christine had glanced at the clock at the exact minute he had arrived. It was nine fifty-eight and she had remarked to herself that he was always bang on time for his arranged visits with their little girl.

And that had been it – no warning, no indication, nothing. Since then her world had been frozen, her heart broken with yearning for her child, and her mind tortured with imagining what Chris might have told her. Looking back, little things should have alerted her: clothing and toys had been left behind when she returned from her nights with her father. But there was no way she could have known he would do this – that he would be capable of such cruelty.

Christine had met Chris, a maths teacher from Fermoy, in Cork, when she had been in her early thirties. A whirlwind romance had resulted in her pregnancy with Deirdre. From early in the relationship she had known he wasn't quite right. He had regular mood swings and often seemed paranoid or upset about nothing. After Deirdre was born, they had struggled on but it was obvious that the relationship wasn't going to last. They had broken up in December 1998 when their daughter was three years old. But they had remained on reasonably good terms, or so Christine had thought, and he had appeared to be happy enough with the visitation rights they had agreed.

The previous August they had even set aside their differences to celebrate Deirdre's fourth birthday. Christine had made a cake in the shape of a doll and they had taken her with four of her little friends to McDonald's. Deirdre stayed overnight with her father regularly at his home in Glounthaune, and the three had been on holiday together. But just before Chris and Deirdre had gone missing, she had refused to allow him take their child on a trip he was planning to Holland – she was too young and Christine didn't want her to be away for so long. Was that why he had done this?

It was a cold Friday morning on 4 December 1999 when Chris Crowley arrived at his estranged partner Christine

O'Sullivan's house in Douglas to collect his daughter for an overnight stay at his house. Nothing was unusual, and Deirdre was delighted to be heading off on an adventure of sorts with her father. Initially, when they failed to come back the next day at the agreed time of five o'clock, Christine had thought they had been in a car accident and had rung the hospitals and police stations, but as the time ticked by, she eventually realised she was going to have to report her daughter missing.

Initially officers had told her that in cases of parental abduction, the problem was usually resolved within one or two weeks, and she would soon have her daughter back. It hadn't taken long before gardaí realised though that this was no ordinary parental abduction and that Chris Crowley had no intention of returning any time soon. In fact, he had laid meticulous plans to disappear without trace. As they probed his bank accounts and made enquiries at the school where he taught, Fermoy's Loreto Convent, it emerged that he had left a sick note to cover his absence for a number of weeks. He had sold his house in Cork, taken out a loan and cashed in a £27,000 insurance policy. It also became worryingly apparent that he had stockpiled the clothes and toys he had 'forgotten' to return to Christine, and they were missing too.

Six days later there was a reported sighting of Chris and Deirdre in the Mitchelstown area of Cork but, despite exhaustive investigations, it couldn't be confirmed. Within a week of the abduction Christine appeared on RTÉ's *Crimeline* programme and begged Chris to bring her daughter back. She appealed to the public for help and urged everyone to keep their eyes peeled.

As Christmas approached she did countless interviews for newspapers and radio shows, never refusing an opportunity to have a picture of Deirdre highlighted. 'She must be starting to wonder where her mammy is,' she told journalists. 'The first few days with Chris would have seemed like a holiday and an adventure, but now she must be getting worried.' At the time investigators hoped his red Toyota Starlet car would be the key to finding father and daughter, but it hadn't been spotted since Deirdre had gone missing.

Christine thought of everything that might help officers and liaised with gardaí daily. In one of her first appeals, she asked people to check isolated houses or caravans or anyone renting a house. She focused on the West of Ireland where Chris had taken Deirdre on a camping holiday that summer.

At home and away from the glare of the media, the tears flowed as she clutched the homemade stocking with Deirdre's name carefully sewn across the top. She hoped against hope that her daughter would be at home with her to open her Christmas presents, which had all been bought and wrapped. Deirdre had talked incessantly about the letter she wanted to write to Santa and changed her mind frequently about what she would ask for.

On 28 December Chris Crowley's car was found at the Talbot Hotel in Wexford – a major breakthrough for investigators, who immediately shifted their focus back to the ferry services to determine whether he had taken Deirdre to the UK over the festive season, when the boats were stuffed with visitors coming and going across the waters.

Interpol was alerted and an international search was launched. Officers initially checked all passengers who had travelled between Rosslare and Fishguard. They sat through hours of video footage at the Welsh port but to no avail. Christine, too, feared that Chris had sought refuge in the UK where he might not be so easily recognised. On RTÉ's *News at*

One the following day, she admitted that she hoped he hadn't left Ireland. 'A Wexford hotel is far too close to Rosslare Harbour for comfort, but I'm hoping that maybe he just dumped the car there and that he's actually somewhere else in the country. It's likely that he would use self-catering accommodation, so I would ask everyone to please check who's staying in any apartment, flat or house. If there's anyone matching their description, please contact the garda.'

As the New Year came in Christine appeared on *The Late Late Show* to discuss the case. In Clonmel, in County Tipperary, a twenty-nine-year-old mother of one was sitting at home watching the programme. She was sure she had seen the man and that he had been with a little girl. She picked up the phone and rang Douglas Garda Station. The following morning when officers called her back, she told them that she was sure she had seen the teacher and the little girl at the Emerald Garden Chinese Restaurant in Clonmel, where her husband was manager, about a week before. She hadn't taken particular notice of the little girl, other than that she had seemed a happy child but the man, she was sure, was Chris Crowley, whose picture had been shown on *The Late Late Show*. The officer asked, were there security cameras at the restaurant. There were not. He thanked her for calling and assured her they would get back if they needed more information. She never heard another word.

Midnight, 4 December 1999
They were almost there now and she hoped he would like it. The child was asleep in the back of the car, but he was beside her, alert and fascinating. It was almost as if he had cast a spell. He had called her 'Bunny'. He was giving her instructions now and she must concentrate, so she would do everything right.

The cash was for food, drink and toys. She must be careful where she shopped. She must phone his mother and tell her all had gone well. She must use the new mobile, never her landline. She must be very, very careful that she wasn't seen. She must keep their secret.

For Christine, the weeks melted into months and the hunt for Deirdre continued. Any hopes that she and the investigation team had that they might still be in Ireland were fast fading. Christine decided to move her hunt to the UK, and in May 2000 she journeyed to Wales, where she made TV and radio appeals for help in finding her daughter.

In Ireland, investigators were making painstaking checks of tens of thousands of telephone calls. One person they were interested in was a young woman by the name of Regina Nelligan, a former pupil of Crowley, who, they had been told, had had a passionate affair with the maths teacher. Among the countless calls that they discovered had been made to her mobile, there had been a number from a phone box in Clonmel. Further checks uncovered how she had been ringing estate agents in the area. Interestingly, friends of Crowley in Cork had been calling a public phone box near her Rialto flat.

By 11 August 2000 Christine was spending Deirdre's fifth birthday still without her little girl. Appeals were launched again through the media and Christine talked about the eight months of hell she had suffered, waiting to see her daughter again. She told Cork-based Barry Roche, who was working for the *Sun* newspaper at the time: 'I'm wondering how she's going to spend her birthday, what presents she's got and how she's feeling. I'm looking at her shoes under her bed at home and I'm thinking they won't fit her any more. She was three feet six inches tall when she went missing. She's probably an inch or two taller now – her dresses mightn't fit her . . . If I thought last December that it would go on for eight months, I would have totally despaired. I don't know how I'd have coped. I pray every morning and night that Deirdre's safe and well.'

Across the country parents held their children tight and said their own little prayers that Deirdre would soon be home with her mother.

In Cork, officers were preparing to interview Regina Nelligan to ascertain if she knew anything about her former lover and where he might be. Nelligan agreed to be interviewed and tearfully admitted that she had indeed had a romantic liaison with her maths teacher but insisted that she hadn't seen him in at least ten years. She said that she had kept the press cuttings about the case, which they had found in her flat, simply because she knew Crowley.

Two months later, she was interviewed again. This time she was more adamant with the officers. 'What kind of a person do you think I am? If I knew where that little girl was, don't you think I would tell you?'

Unfortunately for gardaí, for Christine and for little Deirdre, Regina Nelligan was exactly the type of person she was so insistent that she wasn't. And when officers left her home, she sent a coded message to the man she was so infatuated with that she would literally have given her life for him.

December 2000
It was very dangerous now and she had to be very careful she wasn't seen. The car was stuffed with toys and food, the supplies she brought every six weeks when she got to see him, spend time with him. He had been so brave and she worried for him. She had the Christmas presents for the child, the exact

ones he had asked for. She had wrapped them for him. She knew even before he spoke what he was going to say. She couldn't see him now, not with the police on to her. She could no longer go to the house. It was an emotional parting but he would be in touch again. He would call when he needed her. And she would be there. She loved him more than life itself.

Throughout the year Christine made regular visits to the UK, following up any lead that came in to investigators in Cork. She went to London, Birmingham and Manchester, putting up posters of Deirdre. Every time there was a possible sighting, she hopped onto a plane and packed a bag with photos of her family to show Deirdre how things had changed, and new clothes that would fit her growing girl. But every time, she had to face the long journey back to Cork alone. She set up an Internet site that featured pictures of her daughter and a detailed description of her. She appeared on countless television shows in Britain and in newspapers there too. She even hired a private detective, spending every penny of her savings to try to come up with new leads. She made contact with groups campaigning for missing and abducted children, with Irish groups in Europe, the US, Canada and as far away as Australia, and sent them links to the website and posters of her little girl's face.

By the first anniversary of the disappearance, Christine was struggling to cope, but still she found the strength to continue her campaign to get her daughter back. She went on Pat Kenny's radio show and gave a rare insight into the fear she had about Chris Crowley's mental disorder. 'We're praying for a lucky break – all we can do is pray for a miracle. I think that's all that's going to bring her back. There has to be somebody who knows something – I know Chris Crowley is a very convincing person and he might have persuaded them to believe his stories. But I would plead with them to consider Deirdre – she's just a little girl. She does not deserve to have this done to her. It's gone on far too long. I think Chris sees himself as Deirdre's owner and it's actually okay for him to do this because she belongs to him and to him alone.'

They were strong words and within time would prove to be chillingly accurate and insightful. But they weren't the only words that showed Christine O'Sullivan's maternal intuition was strong and that she could foresee the dangers that lay ahead for Deirdre. At the time she said other things that would prove to be worryingly close to the reality of what was happening in another corner of Ireland, just sixty miles away. In one interview she surmised that because Chris was a fugitive he was living like a hermit: 'Chris will not go out and meet people and obviously neither will Deirdre.' Her insistence on bringing new clothes with her on her trips to the UK, so her child would have something to wear would also prove to be prescient.

As the second Christmas approached, she continued to do anything she could to aid the hunt for Deirdre. She began making a programme with RTÉ for their *Would You Believe* series; she liaised with UK and Canadian investigators to try to get her daughter's image onto the back of milk cartons. And as she lay down to sleep at night, she wondered if she would ever see her again.

At the end of July 2001 RTÉ aired a *Would You Believe* programme focusing on Christine's faith and how it had got her through the dreadful months since Deirdre was snatched. She was a religious woman and had joined the Baptist Church in Cork many years before and regularly attended services there.

Days later, one of the officers heading up the investigation,

Sergeant Brian Fitzgerald of Douglas Garda Station, issued a stern warning against complacency in the abduction of Deirdre. He said that the public were regarding the disappearance as a domestic situation rather than as the criminal act it was. 'If a four-year-old girl was taken by a stranger, the whole country would be up in arms. But because it was her father, people don't seem to be as concerned. They say that the case is sad but tend to think that she is safe with her father.' He appealed for students of the former maths teacher, who might have seen Crowley, to come forward. 'He would have taught maybe fourteen or sixteen thousand students over the years in Fermoy, County Cork. We're hoping that one of these people may have spotted him on their travels.'

While the appeal seemed innocuous to the general public, behind the scenes gardaí were becoming increasingly convinced that Regina Nelligan knew more than she had let on eight months ago when they had interviewed her about her ex-lover Chris. The hunt was beginning to move to Clonmel and the calls they had discovered she had made to estate agents prior to Crowley's disappearance.

30 August 2001, Croan Lodge, Clonmel
The little girl in the ragged clothes played with her dolls as the man paced the room rubbing his forehead. He parted the curtains, looked out of the window, then pulled them shut again. There was a car outside. Two men were getting out and peering at the house. He looked at the child and placed his finger on his lips. 'Don't say a word,' he whispered.

They never had visitors and no one ever called. The last person who had been inside their home was Regina. She had come with the Christmas gifts, all wrapped up. But he had told her not to come again. It was far too dangerous. And he had warned her not to contact him again until she heard from him. But they had been on to her – she had told him so. Twice they had interviewed her. They had asked her questions about Clonmel.

His whole body was wet and beads of sweat were running into his eyes. He raised his shoulder and tugged the sleeve of his T-shirt to dry his face as he waited. It was a determined knock and he knew he had to answer or have them snooping around the back. He needed to buy a little time, just enough to do what he had to do now. He opened the door a crack. They asked him something about trouble with builders and then his name and who he lived with. 'I'm Alan Kaye and I'm the sole resident here,' he said. He knew he hadn't sounded convincing as he slammed the door and went back inside.

This was it. It was either game up – or end this his way.

Moving quickly, he grabbed the gun and loaded it with two cartridges. Now it was time. He had made a promise to himself two years ago when this had begun and he was going to stick to it. Christine would never see her face again. He called her now and she came out to the kitchen, her little sandalled feet slapping on the filthy floor. She stood in front of him. And then he raised the gun.

Outside, the two officers, who had been sent to the little rural cottage outside Clonmel, heard the blasts. One, then a second: two muffled explosions that ripped through the quiet country air. They ran towards the house and tried without success to break down the front door. Then they scrambled around to the back and smashed a window. What they discovered inside would haunt them forever.

In Cork Christine was waiting anxiously for news. What had started as an ordinary day had become a day of hope.

There were developments in the hunt for Deirdre and the gardaí thought they knew where Chris was. They were on their way to a house in Tipperary and, all going well, she might even be reunited with Deirdre that night. She had just put down the phone to Sergeant Dave Treacy, who had been a tower of strength since her daughter had disappeared, and looked for anything to busy herself with until she got further news.

Then Superintendent Brian Calnan called to her house with the news that Deirdre was dead.

That night Christine told journalist Ann Mooney, who was working for the *Irish Daily Mirror*, that she couldn't believe 'her daddy killed her'. 'I never believed they were still in Ireland, I thought they were abroad. I can't believe what has happened. I never believed Chris would hurt my little girl. I just don't believe it – it hasn't sunk in yet. I can't believe I won't see my baby again, especially when we were so close to finding her. I thought I was going to be holding her in my arms this evening and cuddling her and telling her how much I missed her. I wanted her to know how hard I worked to try and find her. Everybody seems to be falling to pieces around me, but it doesn't seem to have sunk in for me, [it's as if] this dreadful thing has happened to some other misfortunate mother.'

At Croan Lodge, gardaí had sealed off the scene, and technical experts were followed by the then State Pathologist, Dr John Harbison. Journalists spoke to locals who said they had never seen a child at the house and hadn't even known it was rented. Some had seen a man but there was no indication whatsoever that a little girl with sparkling blue eyes had ever been in the house.

As officers carried out door-to-door enquiries it soon emerged that Crowley had rarely gone out in the twenty months he had lived there. When he did, he sported a beard and a baseball cap. He had all his supplies delivered and even milkman David Murray, who had been paid forty pounds to deliver milk for three months, had never spotted the child.

Questions were immediately raised about how gardaí had handled the situation and they were forced to defend their actions. They initially set up a press conference in Clonmel, then cancelled it and issued a statement. It read:

> In relation to the deaths of Christopher Crowley and his daughter Deirdre Crowley on 30 August, An Garda Siochana has a duty to carry out a thorough investigation into the full circumstances surrounding deaths of this nature. The Commissioner has appointed a senior officer to examine and investigate all aspects and circumstances surrounding deaths of this nature. When this investigation is complete the file will be forwarded to the coroner so that an inquiry can be carried out by way of inquest.

The statement did not tackle any of the real questions surrounding the officers' approach to Crowley at the door. Chief Superintendent Martin Callanan, then head of the National Bureau of Criminal Investigation and one of the force's most prolific investigators, was appointed to head the internal probe. Alan Shatter TD and Mary Banotti MEP joined the debate. Shatter called on the gardaí to clarify when they had received the report that Crowley was in the house and to explain what planning had been involved in the approach to be taken, should he be discovered there.

Deputy John McGuinness also demanded a garda inquiry into the handling of the case. 'I would be deeply concerned that a man who was as disturbed as Chris Crowley could have been approached as he was.' He questioned the degree to which psychological profiling was used and the level of understanding officers had of Crowley. 'In that instant, approaching the door at the final hour I think may have been a wrong step to take. The man was already frightened, he was already stressed. We need to understand that Chris Crowley had a particular mindset.'

While the gardaí were fielding criticism, the media were making their own inquiries, and the nation wanted to know just how Chris Crowley had hidden out so close to Cork and how he had looked after a child without letting her outside the front door. Regina Nelligan's name soon popped up on the media radar – but just how helpful she had been to Crowley would not emerge for a number of years: until she was brought before the courts for her role in the abduction. What was evident was that she had rented the house for Crowley in the months leading up to the abduction, that she had brought him supplies and that she had had some contact with people in Cork who had also known where the father and child were.

Ballistic experts examined the gun and discovered that it was the one that had been stolen from a caretaker at the school in Fermoy where Crowley had taught.

On 2 September 2001 Deirdre was laid to rest alongside her maternal grandfather Eugene at Kiskeam Cemetery. More than a thousand people gathered at the Church of St Patrick in nearby Ballydesmond, where the white coffin containing the child's body was left closed. On it her mother placed a pair of black patent leather shoes, her favourite Barbie doll, a photograph of the little girl and a candle. Christine was comforted by her four sisters, Therese, Mary, Kathleen and

Noreen. The service was led by parish priest Father Seamus Kenneally, with a chaplain from Cork Institute of Technology, Father Michael O'Regan, and Pastor Terry Price of Christine's Baptist Church.

With tears streaming down her face, Christine managed to find the strength to address the mourners: 'I've prayed that Deirdre would be returned to me and brought home safely. I've prayed to God for her protection and that she would be happy. I trust in God and God knows where she is and what's going on in her life now. God answered my prayers and brought her safely home, not to my home but to His. I am not despairing because I trust in God and I have great hope. I know I will see her again.'

Pastor Price told mourners that he had been privileged to be close to Ms O'Sullivan and her family in their time of such grief and to hear them reminisce about the little girl with the beautiful eyes. Although her life had been terribly short, her mother and family could rely on the fact that God would protect Deirdre and look after them. Father O'Regan read out a short message from Chris Crowley's family, who did not attend: 'We are devastated by the loss of little Deirdre and ask that you convey our heartfelt condolences to Christine and her family at this time. Both she and little Deirdre will always be in our hearts and prayers.'

Christine and her sisters carried the coffin out of the church and into the hearse for the short drive to Kiskeam Cemetery.

The following day, Chris Crowley was to be buried in another part of Cork, separated forever from the little girl he had believed he owned. That morning, local radio chat-show host Neil Prendeville led a discussion about the case, and a clinical psychologist, Dr Colm O'Connor, suggested that in cases like Crowley's, there was often a history of a violent or abusive family. Angela Crowley, Chris's sister-in-law, was outraged. She phoned the station and demanded to be put on air. 'The Crowley family are a very happy, dignified family and his [Chris's] father was one of the most gentle people that I have ever known – it is extremely unprofessional for somebody to come on air and make a suggestion or even hint that, when Chris is being buried today. It's absolutely appalling. There is another side to this story that will come out in the fullness of time and we're not prepared to discuss at this stage, when he's only being buried today. There's a lot more that's gone on here that nobody knows about or probably will know nothing about. We've held our dignity all the way and we don't want his name or his father's name to be taken in such a way on the day of his funeral – it's rubbish in relation to Chris's case, absolutely. What he did, what he did last Thursday, he did out of love and nothing else . . . There's another story and I'm not going to go into it now. It is up to everybody to interpret it as they want, but that's our interpretation of it and we know the full story.'

It was an extraordinary outburst in the wake of such a tragedy.

Dignified as ever, Christine attended this funeral too, at which celebrating priest Michael O'Riordan also said that Chris had acted out of love: 'There is no gain [to describe] the immense suffering at the loss of a little girl who lived just six years of her beautiful life and of Chris, a young man who had so many good things to say and whose life was also cut short. Tenderness and love were part of this. It's obvious that Chris did what he did out of tenderness and immense love, some might say excessive love . . .'

Few who attended the scene of the murder-suicide could agree that there was any sign of love in it. Officers who found father and daughter could see instantly that Chris had shot Deirdre in the face, then stuck the sawn-off shotgun to his own face and pulled the trigger a second time. The child was still wearing clothes she had been taken in. The toes of her shoes had been cut out to make room for her growing feet. The house was damp and dark, and the bedclothes were covered with mildew. And still, incredibly, there was no evidence that Deirdre had ever been outside in all her time there. She had been kept as a prisoner.

As the investigation continued and gardaí prepared a case for the Coroner's Court, officers questioned all of the teachers who worked in the Loreto Convent and quizzed Nelligan three times, in Dublin, Clonmel and Cork. Each time she went willingly.

An inquest was called, as officers continued the criminal investigation into those who might have helped Crowley. It emerged that, while Deirdre had been killed instantly, her father likely survived for several minutes before dying from the massive wound he had inflicted on himself.

Dr John Harbison told of how a garda on duty had briefed him on what to expect when he arrived at the house. He went in through a back door to a kitchen, which was clean but showed signs that a meal had been recently eaten there. In the living room, which was somewhat more untidy, there were toys in a box, and dolls, teddies, a toy radio, crayons and pastels were scattered around. Two shotgun cartridges sat on the sofa.

The two bodies were side by side in the bathroom. Little Deirdre was in a vest and shorts and was lying in a pool of blood, her left leg caught under her father's right. He was still gripping the sawn-off shotgun and had a wound to the left side of his cheek and mouth. Blood was streaming from him across the floor and under a washing-machine. Deirdre's face was unidentifiable. There was a gaping exit wound in her head and her face had been blown away. It had been up to Christine to identify her daughter at St Joseph's Hospital in Clonmel. Superintendent Dick Burke then applied to the coroner, Paul Morris, to have the remainder of the inquest adjourned because medical and identification evidence were incomplete: a file on Regina Nelligan was with the Director of Public Prosecutions, awaiting a decision.

In July 2002 Nelligan was charged with unlawfully detaining Deirdre. At the next sitting of the court in January 2003 she admitted the charge. It was during her sentence hearing that the final parts of the jigsaw and her role in the tragedy would be revealed.

Consultant psychiatrist Dr David Dunne, who had assessed Nelligan, said she was so obsessed with Crowley that she would have done anything for him. In the small courtroom, she sat and listened to the tale of her doomed romance that had ended with the murder of an innocent child.

It had started in 1985, when she was only sixteen and on a school visit to Paris. She had almost missed it but Chris Crowley, her maths teacher, had found her a spot at the last minute. On the bus he had sat beside her and during the trip they had begun their affair. Back in Ireland, in utmost secrecy, they had continued to see each other. She was the daughter of an undertaker and well-known businessman in Fermoy, and Crowley was a respected teacher at the school, liked by his colleagues and his pupils' parents. Nelligan would meet him at his house while his then wife Ursula was out. They explained their meetings away as extra tutorials in maths. She had told psychiatrists that he had made her feel special, confident and strong. He had promised he would leave his wife and move to Dublin with Nelligan when she had finished her Leaving Cert.

Two years later, as she prepared to take up a place at the National College of Art and Design in Dublin, she and Chris had stolen away to Italy. He had changed, though, she had revealed. They had made love just once and he had been cold to her. When they returned, he told her that their plan to set up home was off: he wasn't prepared to give up his wife and career for her.

Any eighteen-year-old would have been upset, but the break-up unleashed a sense of devastation in Nelligan that she would never get over. She thought of killing herself. At one point she travelled to Cork and knocked on his door. His wife was nice to her and took her in for tea, and later Chris drove her back to Dublin. On the way she told him she was going to take her life.

Crowley reacted by spending every weekend for a year in Dublin to keep an eye on her. However, Dr Dunne told the court, 'She got very upset with the arrangement because he was not very kind to her and there was very little sexual contact between them. At times she came close to killing herself and she told him he would have to stop the visits because she could not continue suffering. In his absence, she built him up. He became a hero figure.'

But Crowley was never very far from her mind and she dropped out of college and took a succession of poorly paid jobs, drifting from dingy flat to dingy flat. Crowley's malign influence, Dr Dunne said, left her 'emotionally crippled', and she was unable to form another lasting relationship: no man could match up to Crowley in her mind. For years she drifted on without hearing from him. Meanwhile he had split with his wife and formed a relationship with Christine.

Then, in the summer of 1999, Nelligan received a letter from him, asking her to get in touch. She wrote back and gave him her mobile number. He phoned and arranged to meet her at Portlaoise Shopping Centre where he told her all about his four-year-old daughter Deirdre who, he claimed, was being mentally and physically abused by her mother. He even went as far as to say that Christine was trying to draw his little girl into a religious sect, and while he had always been her carer, he had no hope of winning custody. He told Nelligan he needed her to help him save the little girl. She agreed. The psychiatrist explained: 'He phoned her and told her what to do and she did it immediately. When she arrived, she wanted to talk to him but he told her to get in the car. He took over completely. She was under his control and would dance to his tune automatically.'

In the weeks after the meeting, Nelligan made several trips to Clonmel where he had asked her to rent him a house. She viewed several, but chose the one with no window facing the main road. In November 1999 she had taken out a lease on Croan Lodge, spinning a yarn to the landlord about her partner Alan Kaye.

It also emerged during the sentence hearing that she had bought a mobile phone on 3 December 1999 and had gone to Waterford to await instructions from Chris Crowley. The following evening he had phoned her and told her to meet him in the car park of the Talbot Hotel, where he abandoned his car, introduced Deirdre to his friend 'Bunny' and got her to drive them to Clonmel.

The court also heard how at the house he gave her money and told her to phone his mother and sister to tell them everything had gone well. Four days after his disappearance, he gave Nelligan the phone numbers of two friends and asked her to pass on coded messages to them. Both worked at his school.

Every six weeks Nelligan drove to Clonmel with provisions but was always careful to shop at different locations every time.

She brought toys for Deirdre. Once she had seen Christine pleading on *The Late Late Show* for her daughter's return. When she asked Chris about it, he had become angry and told the trusting Nelligan that Christine's show of love was nothing more than an act. After she had told him gardaí were on to him, he had cut contact with her again and they hadn't spoken in the eight months before he brutally murdered the little girl she had helped him harbour. Dr Dunne said, 'Crowley was a hero figure to her. She built him up and believed she was a better person for knowing him . . . She is in such a bad state that I don't think she is free of him even now. He has become the major figure in her life and she is still mourning him.' Her defence counsel, Niall Durnin SC, appealed for leniency, saying that the influence Crowley had exerted over Nelligan had been in a situation that had gone beyond normal and was not unlike the hold child abusers had over their victims.

Nelligan was given two years for her role in the abduction of Deirdre. The last six months of her prison term were suspended, after Judge Michael O'Shea had considered pleas about the dominant influence Crowley had exercised over her. He ordered that she receive psychiatric treatment while in custody. He also highlighted the suffering caused to Deirdre: 'Deirdre Crowley was deprived of a basic human right – the right to a childhood – over the two-year period. The right to go to school, the right to play with other children, and the love, affection and guidance of her mother Christine were also denied her.'

Outside the court Christine refused to be drawn on the lenient sentence: 'It won't bring Deirdre back,' she said. 'You can't put a value on Deirdre's life. There isn't any sentence that would bring her back or justify her death – you can't make it worth any price. What Chris Crowley did to her was absolutely inexcusable and appalling. He destroyed her life and then continued to destroy my life . . . At the same time, she [Regina Nelligan] was an adult. She made choices and she was given every opportunity to do the right thing and every time she chose not to do so. Now she has to suffer the consequences.'

While Nelligan was put under twenty-four-hour suicide watch in Limerick Prison as she began her sentence, Christine called for others to examine their consciences about their role in what had happened to Deirdre: 'Christopher was obviously a very sick person but there were people out there who were going to work every day, living normal lives with their families around them, living normal social lives, and they had information that could have helped,' she said. 'This should never have happened to Deirdre. She was just an innocent little girl. She did not deserve to be put through this torture.'

She pondered about the man she had once lived with, loved, and for whom she had borne a child – a man who had looked into Deirdre's beautiful blue eyes and then pulled a trigger. 'What was he really like? It seems as if it was another person, as if we didn't really know this person. He was obviously disturbed. He was emotionally crippled – he had this need for control. But I would never have thought he was capable of murder. He used to get mood swings and sometimes he appeared to be a bit paranoid or upset about things. I often think, if only he had been diagnosed as a manic depressive or schizophrenic maybe this would never have happened.'

Perhaps she was right.

4

'YOU ARE MY SUNSHINE'
The Cases of Sharon Grace, Catriona Innes,
Nollaig Owen and Eileen Murphy

The fishermen arrived at their usual spot on Kaats Strand, began to untangle their rods and remove their bait from its boxes. It was a miserable, cold morning, even though it was well into April, and the weather was evidently keeping a few of the regular dog walkers off the strand. But this was the beginning of the flounder season and, despite the pouring rain, there might be some good catch in the grey waters of the Slaney river. It wasn't just locals who used this stretch of water, overlooked by busy Wexford Bridge. It was known throughout the angling world as a mecca for those who enjoyed catching flatfish. In recent times a few anglers had even managed to hook bass and bream.

Some of the group were late, but those who had met for the traditional Sunday get-together were in good form and full of banter. Toddy Roche had just prepared his rods when he spotted something in the shallows, just a few inches from the water's edge. He couldn't quite make it out so he walked towards it. As he crunched over the pebbles, another member of his group saw it too. 'What's that?' he heard, as he stopped in his tracks. He had realised, to his horror, that the strange white object sticking out of the water was a hand. His eyes searched the water and made out a woman and a child, with a toddler, face down, between them. There was no doubt that all were dead. Toddy dialled 999, and within minutes an emergency crew and a team of gardaí had descended on the strand.

From the moment they took the call, it was evident to gardaí in Wexford that the bodies in the water were likely those of Sharon Grace and her two little girls, Mikahla, four, and Abby, three, who had been reported missing by their worried family in the early hours of the morning. Officers had been told that Sharon hadn't been seen since around six p.m. the previous evening, when she had taken a taxi from her home in Pike View, Barntown, four miles from this spot.

Sharon Grace had always been a bright, bubbly person who, for most of her twenty-eight years, had taken on the chin all that life had thrown at her. On more than one occasion she had had to pick herself up and dust herself down. At only seventeen she had been forced to drop out of the Presentation Secondary School in Wexford after falling pregnant with her elder daughter, Amy. She had had to watch her schoolfriends enjoy their teens and early twenties unhampered by motherhood, but she had embraced her new life and loved her little baby more than anything in the world.

From a very close family in Wexford, Sharon was not

rejected for falling pregnant so young and instead was able to rely on her father, Eddy, a well-known athlete, and mother, Rosie, for help during the early days of being a young mother. When she was twenty-one, things started to look up, when she met her future husband, Barry Grace, a base operator at Wexford Cabs. Barry was separated and had a son from his previous marriage, but the couple were thrilled when she became pregnant and had Mikahla in 2001, followed by Abby in 2002. The girls were born a year apart on the same date and Barry used to joke about them being his 'Irish twins'. The couple lived in Pike View, a tiny estate in Barntown, four miles from Wexford town.

The marriage collapsed shortly after Christmas 2003, but Sharon still had the support of her family. Her parents lived less than a mile away, near to the office where Sharon had a job share at Ferns Diocesan Youth Service. Her sister Lilian also lived in Barntown and regularly minded the little girls for Sharon when she was at work.

A year after they had separated, Barry and Sharon were getting on so well that they decided to give their marriage another go. Barry spent more time at the family home and talked about moving back in. But the reconciliation lasted no more than a couple of months and they separated again. Barry took the children on Thursdays and visited every Saturday. As a family they often went out together and, despite the break-up, the couple remained friends.

Every morning Sharon would put her two small daughters into the buggy and walk with ten-year-old Amy to the national school in Barntown. When she wasn't working, she would spend the mornings playing with Mikahla and Abby in the garden or going for walks with them before she went to pick up Amy when school closed for the day. Sharon would often stop and chat with neighbours and their children and was always smiling.

In the weeks leading up to her death, though, Sharon changed. She became withdrawn and uncommunicative with Barry, who found, all of a sudden, that he couldn't get through to her on the telephone and was no longer able to see his children. After a fortnight had passed, he asked social workers if they could help.

'I don't know what changed in her,' his brother Vincent would say later. 'Barry wouldn't have taken the children from her. He didn't want to go to court. All he was looking for was to try and sort out access to the children.' A meeting was arranged between Sharon and a social worker early in April, but it was cancelled. A second was set for the day before she died.

In an interview, Sharon's parents recalled with anguish their daughter's last day. Rosie told the *Wexford People*: 'She rang me and said that one of the social workers had asked her whether she was interested in getting back together with Barry and she had replied, "No." She was told the next step was divorce, but at the time she didn't seem overwrought.' However, when her parents called to her house at two o'clock on 16 April 2005: 'Things were not great there. She was very poorly and upset and looked as if she had been crying all night. Her eyes were red raw. I asked her what was wrong with her and she just started crying. Myself and Ed took the two little girls to the shop to give her a break and when we came back, she was lying on her bed. I joked, "You're lazy, lying on your bed at this time of the day," and she started laughing.'

Sharon got up and talked about lighting a fire and cooking tea for the children. Amy was on a school trip and was expected back at around six o'clock. Her sister Lilian knew Sharon was irrationally worried about her two younger children and whether or not social workers would take them from her and deny her access. She had called at three thirty that day and chatted with her sister, trying to cheer her up. Sharon eventually agreed to have a few drinks with her that night, and before Lilian left, she promised to pick her up a bag of coal and a packet of fags and return at seven thirty. 'Keep your head up,' she told her sister as she left.

When Amy arrived back on Saturday evening the house was empty and she was locked out. Shortly after seven, Lilian arrived to find Amy sitting on the doorstep. She had with her Sharon's coal and cigarettes. Together they went into the house but there was no note and Sharon's handbag was gone. The family rallied around and Rosie and Eddy came straight over. Initially they carried out their own inquiries by knocking on neighbours' doors. One neighbour had thought they saw Sharon leaving in a taxi some time after six. The family tried to phone her mobile but there was no reply and, as the hours wore on, they decided they were going to have to contact the gardaí.

Over the course of the garda investigation, which was conducted for the coroner, it would emerge that Sharon had taken a taxi to Wexford Quays where she walked across the bridge and into Ely Hospital. With her little girls, she had gone to the reception desk and asked to see a social worker. She was told that nobody was on duty as it was the weekend.

According to statements taken from staff at the hospital and local eyewitness accounts, Sharon made no further enquiries and left with the two little girls. She would have walked past the large signs on the walls directing people towards the 'Counselling Service' and past a statue of St Francis of Assisi overlooking the garden. She was seen walking past the Riverbank Hotel next to the Ely Hospital carrying one child while the second was beside her.

The girls must have slowed her over the twenty minutes it would have taken to reach their final destination: they must have been tired and ready for their beds. But instead of bringing them home, Sharon Grace, now a stranger to those who knew and loved her, led them down a narrow country road that ended in Kaats Strand. The beach was deserted when she left her handbag on the shore and walked with the two children into the sea. Fishermen would later speculate that she must have had to wade fifteen feet into the freezing water, clutching her children on either side. Then she held them under until they stopped gasping for air before drowning herself.

Normally it would take the tide six hours to come back in but on that evening, by some freak of nature, just five minutes later the three bodies were washed back to the shore. They were still together when they were found the following morning.

Throughout that night Sharon's phone would have rung incessantly on the shoreline. Those who loved her and her little girls were trying desperately to contact her – her disappearance on that Saturday evening was so out of character. Barry Grace was on a weekend away in Cork with his brother Vincent when he had a call in his hotel room at two a.m. from Sharon's mother. She told him that the family were very worried because Sharon and the girls had been missing since earlier that evening and they were going to have to telephone the gardaí and report her missing. He stayed up all night dialling her mobile phone.

Early the following morning, Vincent drove his brother back to Wexford. By the time they hit Waterford, Sharon's phone was no longer ringing: either it had been switched off or the battery had run out. By the time the brothers were arriving at New Ross, Barry had phoned Sharon's mother again. He knew something was very wrong.

On the outskirts of Wexford they turned off to Barntown and the narrow road to the Reddys' home, where shocking news awaited Barry. Just an hour before, the family had been sitting together when a car pulled up with two detectives and a priest in it. Vincent said later, 'It was lashing rain. I said, "We'll wait for you." I drove a hundred yards up the road to turn the car around. It was a narrow road. When we drove back down, I saw Barry coming out of the gate. He was holding his head in his hands. He stopped and stood in the middle of the road in the lashing rain, holding his head, saying, "No, no, no." I got out of the car. He told me Sharon and the kids were dead . . . He told me that Sharon walked down the beach and into the water.'

As the family tried to come to terms with the deaths, the three bodies were removed from Kaats Strand and gardaí were preparing a statement for the media, indicating that they believed there was nothing suspicious about the three deaths. From the outset it was evident that the young mother had killed her little girls before taking her own life, and by the following afternoon, the State Pathologist, Dr Marie Cassidy, could confirm that all three had died from drowning.

As far as an investigation went, it was cut and dried, but detectives still had to prepare a case for the coroner and questions had to be answered as to Sharon's last movements, and why a young mother would see so little hope left in life that she would choose to kill her children.

Lilian gave a brief insight to Sharon's mental state when she said that she was unhappy at the involvement of social workers with her kids: 'She didn't want to go through the courts system, social workers and all that. She felt distraught. The kids were upset as well. I knew she was upset, but I never thought for a second it was playing on her mind that much,' she told the *Irish*

Times. 'She was very worried about her children and whether she was going to have access to them. She just didn't want to leave them. She was in bad form since Thursday: she wasn't in her right mind. The last time I saw her was at three thirty p.m. on Saturday. We were planning to have a few drinks that night and she asked me to bring home a bag of coal and a packet of fags. I never saw her again after that.' Despite Sharon's evident distress, there could have been no indication that she was capable of doing what she was about to do.

At the funerals, Amy was inconsolable. Tears poured down her cheeks as the bodies of her mother and sisters were removed to St Alphonsus Church in Barntown. At the altar they lay side by side, Sharon in an open coffin, her expression calm, while her two daughters were lightly veiled with white silk. Cuddly toys were placed in their coffins. It was up to local parish priest Father Sean Gorman to try to make sense of what had happened.

'It is not a time for judgement,' he told the congregation. 'We can have feelings of guilt, we can ask questions like, did we let Sharon down, could we have said or done something that could have prevented this tragedy? And also we can have feelings of anger that Sharon chose to leave us so suddenly. We could have feelings of despair – has a day ever been this dark before, will the sun ever shine again? Nobody really knows what is in our hearts. Only God Himself knows. He understands us better than we understand ourselves. That is why he has reserved for Himself, and Himself alone, the right to judge.'

While the priest urged mourners not to judge Sharon Grace, anger was rising in Wexford that its support services for those in mental anguish were far from adequate. There had been seven suicide-related deaths in the county within four days, and Sharon's visit to Ely Hospital on the night of her death was about to become public. Days after the funeral, Eddy Reddy made an emotional outburst, saying that his daughter had been refused help: 'My Sharon was looking for someone, looking for help and couldn't get it. We will never ever forget that for the rest of our lives. The image of her wandering around, looking for someone from whom she could get help will be with us for the rest of our lives. When we found out that she had called to Ely Hospital and got no one, we were even more shattered. If someone had brought her in, sat her down, given her a cup of tea and chatted with her, it might have changed her mind. But there was nobody on and nobody there to help her.'

The Wexford Health Executive reacted by announcing plans to improve suicide-prevention services in the light of the drownings. It insisted that the hours of a clinical nurse specialist would be extended from the normal working week until one a.m. seven days a week in the A&E department at Wexford General Hospital.

Incredibly, seventeen months later it emerged that, despite the drownings, there were still no emergency social work facilities available in Wexford outside office hours. It seems that nervous breakdowns still have to happen between nine and five.

The inquest heard about Sharon's visit to Ely Hospital. The receptionist on duty, Marion Redmond, told the inquest that Sharon had come in at seven thirty p.m. with her children. She told a shocked Coroner's Court: 'She asked to speak to a social worker. I told her there were none at the hospital. She asked for an emergency number but I did not have one. I offered to contact Wexford General Hospital for one, but she said not to bother. At eight ten p.m. I saw the woman walking towards Castle Bridge carrying one child in her arms with the other one walking behind her.' Asked by the coroner, Jimmy Murphy, if emergency numbers had since been put at Reception, she replied, 'No,' to gasps from those present. 'So nothing has been learned,' the coroner observed.

As the jury considered its verdict, the foreman Sean Meyler said the fact that procedures had not changed at the hospital was an insult to the memory of those who had died. Mr Murphy agreed: 'It is incredible that this lady went into this hospital, crying for help and the reception did not have emergency numbers. The loss of innocent lives should never have occurred.'

After the inquest, Sharon's father said he was sickened by Social Services: 'It is an absolute scandal, that's what it is. Social Services should be ashamed of themselves ten times over. A young girl goes for help and is told to come back on Monday. The country is awash with money, but for the ordinary Joe Soap there is nothing.'

Two years after Sharon's death, local services would again come in for severe criticism, when father-of-two Adrian Dunne smothered his children, strangled his wife and hanged himself in their rental home. He carried out his murder-suicide at the weekend. The families hadn't known one another, but two years after the death of Sharon and his children, Barry Grace would join Adrian's mother Mary in a march on the Dáil demanding a 24/7 on-call social worker.

Sharon Grace must have known something was wrong with her when she sought help at Wexford Hospital. Her family knew that she had fallen into a deep depression in the weeks leading up to her death. In hindsight too, too few can claim that the warning signs were anything but plain to see in the weeks before Adrian Dunne killed his family. But there was little if nothing to indicate what Catriona Innes was about to do the weekend that her daughter Caitlin celebrated her first Holy Communion. Twenty-six-year-old Catriona, known to her family as 'Triona', gave no warning that she was capable of the murder-suicide that left a nation baffled.

Catriona came from a family of six and was the second eldest of four girls and two boys. Her mother, Winnie, was a housewife, and her father, Greg, had served at Finner Military Camp in Ballyshannon. Originally from the seaside resort of Bundoran in Donegal, Catriona had been a spirited, adventurous girl who loved nothing better than the great outdoors. She longed to travel but when she became pregnant at eighteen, her future was mapped out. Catriona had little contact with the father of her child, but with the support of her close-knit family, she made a life for herself and her baby girl Caitlin and settled into it.

Initially she lived in Bundoran, where she worked in many of the town's restaurants and later at hotels, including the Allingham Arms, the Holyrood and the Great Northern. When Caitlin was four, they moved to Letterkenny and Catriona got a job working at McNutt's wool and cashmere outlet. Caitlin started school at the local Scoil Mhuire Gan Smal, where she was loved by all who knew her. She was a bright little girl, who skipped off to school every day on the local bus, which swung by the little council house on its way around the area.

In recent years Triona's parents had decided to live apart but they had remained on good terms and she had continued to see both. They loved her little girl dearly. Her father remained at the family home in Drumacrin Avenue, while Winnie moved to a picturesque new cliff-top estate two miles south of Bundoran.

By May 2007 things were looking up for Triona and her daughter. Caitlin was in the second class at school and was looking forward to making her first Holy Communion, while Catriona had landed a new job, which would pay her another few quid a week to help with the bills. Even better, she was finally to be given the keys to a new council house where she hoped to settle down for good. Catriona had told friends she was really looking forward to moving into her new home, but she had also indicated that she found life a bit tough. She didn't complain, but few could imagine it would be easy to bring up a child single-handedly while trying to work. An on-off relationship she was having with a local man was also on the rocks again, but apart from that, nothing in the life of the young mother and her daughter gave anyone cause for concern.

Three weeks before Caitlin's first Holy Communion day, Donegal and the rest of the country were in shock at the death of a young family in Wexford. Ciara O'Brien, from Burt, which was twenty miles from Letterkenny, had been found dead along with her two little girls and her husband Adrian, after an apparent murder-suicide pact. The case had received huge coverage across the country and many of the parents at Caitlin's school had spoken in hushed tones about the tragedy. For the children of the second class, though, the only things on their minds were white dresses and hairdos.

Little Caitlin was no different. She loved to dress up and had been talking about her own Communion for weeks. Her dress was a family heirloom: it had once been her aunt's wedding gown before it was remodelled into a beautiful white dress that Caitlin would wear for her big day on Saturday, 12 May. Catriona had great plans for the weekend, and had arranged for her own parents to come along for the ceremony at St Eunan's Cathedral before they would all go for a meal. The Sunday, too, would be a day of celebration for little Caitlin, and as a treat, Catriona had promised to bring her to the amusements in Bundoran.

The weekend had started full of promise. Catriona finished work on Friday afternoon and collected the keys for her new council house on the outskirts of Letterkenny, before heading home to get an early night. The following morning, Caitlin had woken early and excited. She had her hair done just the way she wanted it, then changed into the dress, and put a sparkling tiara on her head. She looked like a princess.

For Caitlin the day was everything she had imagined. She had lined up in her dress for photographs with her classmates after the ceremony, then headed for the meal with her grandparents, Greg and Winnie, and her mother. The next day she put on her dress again and headed with her mum to Bundoran, where more photographs were taken of her on the beach and where, after she had changed, they went to the funfair.

After a tiring day, Catriona and Caitlin headed for home. When they arrived, Catriona texted her mother to say they were safely back at the house. At nine thirty she had a conversation with Winnie and admitted she was feeling 'fed up' and was going to bed. When Winnie asked if she wanted to talk about her problems, she replied, 'Not tonight, please.' Officers would later discover that she had made another call shortly afterwards to her on-off boyfriend, but it had gone unanswered and she hadn't left a message.

On Monday morning school-bus driver Cathal McGettigan called to the house as usual to collect Caitlin. The car was parked outside but there was no sign of anyone, so he blew the horn and waited for about five minutes until he decided the little girl must be taking a day off and drove on towards the school. On Tuesday morning he returned, but still there was no reply.

In the meantime Catriona's friend Caroline Gallagher had become concerned. Caroline had seen Catriona at the First Holy Communion and thought she was in good form. When she hadn't seen mother and daughter for three days, she called to the house. The blinds were down and the car was parked outside. She rang the doorbell, then phoned her friend's mobile. She could hear it ringing inside but it wasn't answered. Peering through a window, she could see a wallet on the kitchen table and a child's school uniform neatly pressed and hanging on a door.

Later that afternoon, she had a call from Catriona's employers, who were worried because she hadn't turned up for work, and it appeared that Caitlin hadn't been back at school. Caroline phoned Winnie and then called the gardaí.

It was Tuesday afternoon when two officers forced their way into the little home at Whitethorn Close in Letterkenny. Within seconds of gaining entry they found Catriona hanging by the neck. It was clear she had been dead for some time. A female garda made her way upstairs and entered a room with a single bed and an array of toys. On the bed, wearing her nightclothes, lay Caitlin. She, too, was dead.

For those who knew Catriona, it was hard to believe what had happened. It was clear that after Caitlin had settled down to bed after her big weekend, her mother had inexplicably gone into her room and placed a pillow over her face. She had smothered her before returning downstairs to hang herself.

Dr Jim McDaid attended the scene and pronounced both mother and daughter dead at the house. He would later say that it was the saddest and most distressing scene he had ever attended as a doctor. They had not been his patients but he had been told they were a perfectly normal young mother and daughter. The house was well-kept and you could see that

Caitlin wanted for nothing.

At Caitlin's school, a shocked staff tried to continue as normal to minimise the impact of the tragedy. Principal Roisin Ui Fhearraigh issued a brief statement: 'She was a lovely child. The family need our support and prayers at the moment. These are very sad and tragic circumstances, and our prayers and thoughts are with the family at this time. The school community will continue to pray for all those affected by this very sad and tragic event.'

Neighbours were stunned and nobody could throw any light on what could possibly have driven Catriona to do such a thing. As locals searched for answers, Dr McDaid suggested that the case might have been a copycat murder-suicide of the Dunne-O'Brien tragedy. He had acted as a spokesman for the O'Brien family and had a good knowledge of psychiatric disorders. He also said, to TV3, that other families could be at risk: 'The reality of the situation is that they [infanticides] normally occur in batches. There is a type of copycat connotation to this one as well. It is sometimes difficult for anyone to see the warning signs ahead of such tragedies. According to the neighbours, the little girl was very popular in the neighbourhood and there were no outward signs that anything was wrong at all. You just don't understand what goes on in the mind of some of these people . . . There's a lot of things going on behind closed doors that we're not aware of.'

That night Caitlin lay in a small white coffin at her grandmother Winnie's home, her mother beside her in an oak coffin. The bodies had been brought from Letterkenny to Bundoran in two hearses, with a garda escort for the fifty-mile journey. Businesses closed their doors and people lined the streets as a mark of respect. The following day, when they were laid to rest, Bundoran parish priest Father Raymond Munster echoed Dr McDaid's sentiments when he said that Catriona must have been suffering from some form of undiagnosed depression: 'We will never be able to understand the pressure Catriona felt in the days and weeks which have gone by . . . The pressure which overturns normal life and forces a mother to bypass what is normal and maternal is indeed baffling for every single one of us. The lack of interest in one's own life, however successful it may seem to others, is something most of us are unable to understand. I feel we must conclude that pressure and depression contributed greatly to this situation. The events which sadden us so greatly today can only be the result of an illness which was difficult to detect and suddenly came to light with devastating and terrible results.'

Catriona's family, her sisters Amanda, Tricia and Charlene, her brothers Greg Junior and Tommy, with Winnie and Greg, sat grim-faced and held one another.

'We should not fool ourselves that in times of difficulty, we can get by without seeking the help of others when we may need it,' the priest warned.

After the funeral Winnie requested a meeting with Fine Gael leader Enda Kenny when she heard he was canvassing in the area. She asked him for a pledge that he would do all he could to ensure adequate services were made available to people who felt suicidal or depressed. In the week after the funeral, she insisted that she had seen no outward signs of distress in her daughter: 'There wasn't a hint from Triona, not the slightest indication, that anything was wrong. We had spent a lovely weekend together. Caitlin spoke non-stop about the dress . . . She talked for weeks about the dress before the big day. She got a new tiara and she thought that she was a little princess. She just loved it all. She was a real dressy-up little girl. She loved style. She loved appearance. She had her hair done that morning the way she wanted to. She was a really outgoing little girl, a real jolly girl.'

At the inquest, Coroner Sean Cannon said that to take the life of a child was 'beyond human reason', and that it was everyone's responsibility to tackle the epidemic of suicide and self-harm.

His words and Dr McDaid's warning were still echoing across the nation when yet another mother did the unthinkable in a County Cork river. In July 2007 Nollaig Owen strapped her nine-month-old baby Tadhg into his pushchair, before overturning it in the Araglin river in Kilworth. She had earlier sung 'You Are My Sunshine' to the little boy as she prepared him for a walk. The pair were found within hours of the tragedy, when a passer-by saw the bodies in the water and raised the alarm.

Unlike Catriona Innes, who had apparently given nobody any indication of what she was going to do, Nollaig, aged thirty-three, was a huge cause of concern to her family and particularly her husband, Gareth. She had developed a very severe form of post-natal depression after the birth of her only son, Tadhg. It was so bad that the couple had moved from their home in South Africa back to Ireland just weeks previously to be near her family, so she could have the support her husband felt she needed. He had also hoped that her mother and siblings would urge her to get professional help.

Nollaig had grown up in Kilworth in a large family who were well-known in the area. Her late father, Donal Kenneally, had owned a construction firm in the town and the family had also run a pub. Nollaig had three sisters and four brothers, and their home was known for its open door to anyone who called. She was friendly and caring and loved to go out. Before she had her baby, there was no indication that she might be a candidate for severe post-natal depression.

Nollaig had met Gareth when he worked at BUPA Ireland, in Fermoy. After they married, they moved to his native South Africa and settled in Johannesburg. Nollaig often flew home to see her family and she also entertained the many visitors who made the trip to see her. Tadhg had been born the previous November and, from the outset, it was obvious that all was not right with Nollaig. Weeks after the birth she complained about being utterly exhausted – far beyond the type of tiredness most new mothers experience from broken sleep and the tough new routine a baby requires. She was unsettled and wanted to move closer to her home. When Gareth lost his job in South Africa and got a new one in the UK, they moved there. The exhaustion continued and Nollaig saw a doctor who diagnosed her with post-natal depression.

Closer to home, Nollaig frequently flew to Cork and spent plenty of time with her family and friends. But Gareth felt she needed a more permanent move to Ireland, and two weeks before the tragedy, she had gone back to her family and was waiting for Gareth to join her. He hoped that, among her loved ones, she might seek the psychiatric help she so badly needed.

A week before she strapped her son into his pushchair that fateful day, Nollaig had made a suicide attempt by drug overdose. Her family had begged her to get professional help but she had refused. That Friday, Gareth flew to Cork to spend the weekend with his wife and child. He knew nothing of her attempted suicide. The following Saturday morning she said she was going out for a walk. But she didn't return after an hour and a half, when little Tadhg would have been due his bottle. Gareth and her family became extremely anxious. They were out searching for them when the bodies were spotted by a passer-by.

During her funeral mass, Gareth said that when his wife walked into his life he had found 'my sun, moon, my everything'. He said the birth of Tadhg had made his life complete, and described his and Nollaig's excitement when they had found out they were expecting a little boy: 'We bought two pregnancy tests to be sure. To hear his heartbeat for the first time was like an echo of our love . . . My sense of loss knows no bounds. My whole world lies before me in a wooden box. Family no more. Its place in the universe snuffed out. My grief and pain has no limit. My universe has come to an end – I am all alone. Nollaig and Tadhg, sleep tight. I love you so much.'

Nollaig's mother, Peggy, gave an insight into her daughter's caring nature: she talked about how kind Nollaig had been to her late father, Donal, after he had been paralysed in an accident. She had wound down his business and put a 'huge effort' into looking after him. She said she had seen at 'first hand the love Nollaig had for her son', but that unfortunately she hadn't come through the post-natal depression from which she was suffering.

Parish priest Father Donal Leahy said Nollaig's grief-stricken relatives shouldn't second-guess themselves about what they could have done to prevent the tragedy. 'For whatever reason, Nollaig's pain was too much for her to bear,' he said, and reminded mourners that she had once climbed mountains in Italy to raise funds for the mental-health charity Aware.

Her death and its timing, so close to those of the Dunnes in Wexford and the Inneses in Donegal, sparked a national debate about murder-suicide and spurred the Irish Association of Suicidology to issue a statement about post-natal depression, a much neglected condition in Ireland: 'Post-natal depression is very common and it's often dismissed as "baby blues" and as something quite natural. Very severe psychiatric illnesses can develop during pregnancy and childbirth, and people need to be aware of this,' said Dr John Connolly, secretary of the IAS. 'Making people get help is a very difficult issue. It's difficult to get people to get help if they don't want it.' The Association also warned that psychiatric services for many in distress were remote and not user-friendly. It said that a number of factors in familicides included post-natal depression, relationship problems and loneliness. 'Some of these tragic events are probably not preventable. They do, however, raise many questions about issues related to suicide, suicide prevention and the promotion of positive mental health.' It pointed to a lack of specialist psychiatric services for women during pregnancy and in the year following childbirth, and an inadequate level of assessment for children during that period.

Aware, which aims to defeat depression, issued a warning to those suffering from an illness similar to the one that spurred Nollaig to kill herself and her baby. It said that there are two forms of post-natal depression, which may arise some weeks after a baby is born. The first is similar to general depression, while the second is a more serious form known as puerperal psychosis, which develops six weeks after a birth. While rare, it affects about one in every five hundred mothers and is a biological or chemical form of mood disorder, similar to manic depression. In the majority of cases, the mother's ability or desire to look after her child is severely affected. A mother who is very depressed can harbour strong suicidal ideas or, less frequently, an impulse to kill her own child. Unfortunately, Nollaig fell into the final category, and the impulse overtook her before anyone could stop her.

* * *

Eileen Murphy and her four-year-old son Evan checked into the Skeffington Arms Hotel in Galway City Centre on a cold January day in 2007. It was well after Christmas, the time of year when everyone could do with a holiday to break the long grim days of winter.

Eileen was twenty-six, a single mother who worked hard to keep her home in Cork where Evan had everything a little boy could want. As she filled in the hotel registration form he played excitedly in the reception area, tugging at his mother's sleeve while she spoke to receptionist Lisa Moore. They were to spend a few days in Galway and Eileen wanted to know about getting to the Cliffs of Moher. While they had missed that day's excursion on the bus tour, they could buy tickets in a nearby shop for the following day.

The next morning Eileen and Evan were up early and she bought their tickets in the shop beside the hotel. Shop assistant Ann Koshiba was well used to the tourists coming in for tickets for the day-long tour, which took in other attractions, such as the famed Ailwee Caves. Most asked what time the bus returned to Galway but Eileen Murphy did not.

At the bus stop the pair queued with the group of thirty or so tourists, including Americans, Chinese and a large group from Limerick on a long weekend break. They were quiet and unassuming, and Eileen certainly looked younger than she was. She was tall and very slim, while Evan was a big child for his age. As the doors opened and the group piled on, Eileen led Evan by the hand and the pair took their seats at the back of the coach.

Spirits were high, and it was a clear, crisp day, perfect for the Cliffs. They were assured that they would have a fantastic view of the majestic rock rising sheer from the Atlantic Ocean. As the tour got under way, the driver began to banter with the group as he told them where they would be going and what sort of things they could expect to see. Along the road, he made jokes and pointed out areas of interest. Some tried to make conversation with Eileen but, while she wasn't rude, she had no interest in engaging with her fellow passengers. And as the bus wound its way out of Galway and into the countryside, she didn't point out the sights to the little boy. When she did speak, it was simply to ask when they would get to the Cliffs of Moher.

Around midday the bus pulled in for the first of the many attractions at the Ailwee Caves. Among the oldest in Ireland, the caves are made up of 3,400 feet of underground passages that lead into the heart of the mountain and contain a river and a waterfall as well as celebrated stalactites and stalagmites. They are one of the region's top tourist attractions, but for Eileen they held little appeal.

The group piled out, draped with cameras, and were brought on a tour of the decorated caverns. Inside, Eileen struggled with Evan, who became agitated and frightened when the lights were turned off. She left the group, brought him outside and bought him a bag of crisps and some 7-Up as she waited for the bus to get going again.

Back on the bus Evan continued to fidget, and many noted that Eileen had to regularly reprimand him. He was obviously a spirited little boy but nobody guessed that he had special needs and behavioural problems.

The driver made his way through Ballyvaughan and passed the little village of Fanore before he pulled into Doolin, where the group disembarked for lunch at O'Connor's pub. Eileen and Evan sat alone and she ordered him a plate of chips but he didn't eat them. Before they left, she asked a waitress to pack them up for him.

As the group gathered to get back on the bus, Eileen made her way to the front of the queue and, instead of taking their seats at the back, she sat down behind the driver right at the front. The couple who had occupied the seats previously stopped briefly but thought better of causing a fuss and moved on.

Minutes later the bus pulled into the car park at the Cliffs of Moher visitor centre. While the group chatted and organised their cameras, Eileen disembarked and started to head off up the road. The driver called after her to be careful.

Aine O'Loughlin was one of the rangers on duty that day, and noticed the young woman walking determinedly towards the top of the cliffs. She was carrying the child and, although it was a gusty day, was making her way very purposefully towards an edge. As O'Loughlin watched, she saw the woman ignore one of the many signs warning visitors not to go beyond that point. She called another ranger, Tom Doherty, to go after them: they had appeared to make their way onto one of the more dangerous cliff edges and had now disappeared from view.

Tourists and thrill-seekers often ignore the signs dotted all over the cliff edges to get a closer view of the drops. Locals were often stunned by the number of people willing to risk their lives to take photographs, not realising that the edges could collapse under them. But with the winds gusting, this was no day for anyone to venture out beyond the walkways – especially not someone with a young child in tow.

As Aine asked her colleague to search the cliff edge for the woman and the little boy, another visitor reported that they had heard a child crying. Tom went up to where Aine had last spotted the pair but he couldn't see anyone on or around the cliff edge. He made his way nearer to the sheer 600-foot drop and looked down into the sea. In the waters below he saw a woman and a child. He immediately alerted the lifeboat and other rescue services that there had been an accident on the cliffs. The Doolin lifeboat, located just down the coast, was immediately mobilised and went straight to the area where the bodies had been seen floating in the water.

When they pulled her from the icy Atlantic, Eileen Murphy was dead but Evan was still alive and they did what they could to save the little boy, as a helicopter arrived to transfer them to University College Hospital. By the time it had touched down on the helipad, Evan had died from the horrific injuries he had received during the fall. State Pathologist Dr Marie Cassidy would later find that both had died from fractures of the spine.

The news was numbing. Over the years, there had been many deaths on the Cliffs, some accidental, others not. But, until now, there had been none of a parent and child.

That evening a garda and a priest knocked on a door in Churchtown, in County Cork, where Eileen's parents, Eileen and Liam, were blissfully unaware that the news they had heard earlier about two people falling from the Cliffs of Moher concerned their daughter and grandchild.

In Effin, Limerick, Simon Meade, Evan's father and Eileen's estranged partner, was also about to hear the news. Although the couple had separated, Simon, a painter and decorator, lived a few miles from their home in Ballyhea and was extremely active in Evan's life.

Neighbours at Eileen's neat council home in Corrin Drive, North Cork, told reporters that they were stunned by the actions of the quiet, unassuming mother whose child had played football on the street and seemed happy. Eileen had moved into the estate just two years ago. Nobody could throw any light on why she had apparently jumped from the Cliffs and taken little Evan with her. The pair had settled into their home and Evan, a Liverpool fan, had made friends easily. He had a trampoline in the back garden and children from the estate had spent the previous summer playing with him. They remembered Eileen as a private person but someone who always smiled and waved at them. Evan, many said, was a hyperactive child but easy enough to manage. He was due to start in the local national school the following September and was making great strides in his pre-school, where he was the only special-needs pupil. Evelyn O'Keefe, a teacher described him as 'a bubbly young boy . . . Evan was a very popular little boy. He was a wonderful, cheerful, energetic four-year-old.' At the Kostal factory, located just a few miles from Mallow, where Eileen had worked for six years, she was described as 'a highly valued member of staff'. Colleagues were shocked.

As the days wore on, reports indicated that Eileen had left a suicide note with just two words – 'I'm sorry' – but it later emerged that there was no letter. There was also speculation that she had suffered from depression but had hidden it from her neighbours and colleagues. Those who were on the tour bus said she had been anxious to get to the cliffs, and as they had got close to them, she had seemed almost elated.

On the morning of Saturday, 3 February 2007, at their small yellow farmhouse, Eileen's family were trying to prepare themselves for the funerals – but they also wanted to set the record straight. Hours before they buried their daughter and grandson, Eileen Murphy senior gave an interview to the *Sunday Tribune* newspaper in which she vented her fury at media speculation about her family. She insisted there was no suicide note and that Eileen had been happy. 'She was very quiet, but she was happy. She had brains to burn too. A really intelligent girl. She always wanted to go to college, actually, and she was really interested in doing a science course. But she couldn't go, you know, because of Evan . . . We've just been so shocked by everything that's happened and everything that has been written in the papers. No one has asked us for the truth or the right information. They've just done what they want with it. The gardaí were with us when we went into her house, after we heard the news, and there was no note . . . She went to work every day and looked after the little one and played with him, and everything seemed to be fine . . . But she was a very quiet girl anyway. A very deep girl. It is possible that if there was something upsetting her, she wouldn't have talked to us about it, but we didn't think she was unhappy at all.'

Eileen said her daughter was in good form, heading off on her trip. The following day she herself had been in the car when she heard that two people had fallen off the Cliffs. 'They didn't give any names, and I remember thinking that was awful . . . One paper said that she took Evan in her arms and jumped off the cliff. This is wrong. I don't know where they get their information from, but it is wrong.'

Three hours later Eileen, Liam, their son William and their other daughter Valerie stood together in the chapel in Churchtown where two coffins sat side by side, covered with white sheets. Little was said during the funeral about the mother and son, their lives or deaths. The service was stark and sombre, and those who attended left with no explanation about what had happened.

Months later, during the inquest, State Pathologist Dr Marie Cassidy said that Eileen had appeared to jump from the Cliffs. Evidence had been heard of the bus trip and Eileen's apparent dash from the coach once it had pulled in at the Cliffs. Delivering his verdict, West Galway Coroner Dr Ciaran McLoughlin said that both had died at the scene and offered his sympathies to Eileen's family. He also urged Clare County

Council to look at the possibility of increasing the safety measures in place at the Cliffs of Moher, particularly where there was a risk that people might be blown off the cliffs.

But instead of providing answers, Eileen's family said the inquest left them even more confused about the circumstances surrounding the deaths. Eileen senior again spoke to the *Sunday Tribune* : 'I still don't know what happened. I still have unanswered questions. At the inquest, we felt excluded and didn't know what was going on all the time. We had no solicitor because we weren't told we could have one. I complained to the coroner afterwards . . . It's still very hard and of course we're still very upset. There are a lot of rumours going around that aren't true about what happened. Everyone has something different to say about it and we live in a small community. It's not something we'll ever get over. Not knowing exactly what happened makes it even harder. At this stage, we probably never will.'

5

MURDER MOST FOUL
The Cases of Mary Keegan, Lynn Gibbs and Ruth Murphy

Mary Keegan was an ordinary girl-next-door, whose life appeared to follow the well-worn trail of countless women – growing up, falling in love, marrying and making a comfortable nest for two little children. But one day, something would turn Mary into an unrecognisable monster.

Mary had grown up in Rathfarnham, a middle-class Dublin suburb, with her brother John and sister Patricia. The Flynns lived on Anne Devlin Road and the children had a secure, stable and loving childhood. Mary's father, John, was a builder, and her mother, Betty, a nurse. As a teenager, Mary had met Brian Keegan, who lived a few streets away at St Enda's Park. He was one of twins, whose mother had died in childbirth, and his father had reared the family. The couple dated, and were married in 1992 at the Church of the Holy Spirit in Ballyroan.

Mary worked for the finance company GE Capital Woodchester while Brian, a mechanic, was with a local garage until he got a high-powered job with a firm that sold garden machinery, which he often sourced abroad and tested. Life was good, and by the time their first son, Glen, was born in 1996, they had moved into a three bedroom semi-detached house in Firhouse, not far from their own family homes. In 2000, baby Andrew arrived, and the family was complete.

Mary and Brian were a sociable couple and their weekends revolved around ferrying their boys to football matches and cheering them on from the sidelines of St Enda's GAA club, where Glen was a rising star. Many believed he would be chosen for the Dublin senior team as soon as he became of age. He loved rugby too, and his younger brother seemed to be following in his footsteps on the sports field. The family liked to walk in the mountains and the hills that surrounded their home. Mary was neighbourly and involved herself in her community, forging strong friendships with the other mothers who lived in Killakee Walk. They would regularly have one another's children in to play, and chat over coffee when they called to collect them.

Brian travelled abroad regularly on business, so it wasn't unusual that in February 2006 he had to spend a week in the US, sourcing machinery for the upcoming Ryder Cup, which was due to be held at the K Club in Kildare the following September. His firm, Brodericks, had been awarded the contract for the cutting equipment that would bring the fairways up to standard for the golfing extravaganza. Mary never worried about being at home alone, and anyone who met her in the days leading up to the tragedy said she was her usual cheerful, busy self.

On the evening of Friday, 10 February, Mary and the boys

got into the car and made the short trip to see her parents. She was close to them and they loved to see their two young grandsons. She was in great form and looking forward to the following morning when she planned to cheer on Glen, who was playing a match against local rivals Ballinteer St Johns.

On the Saturday morning she rose early, bundled Andrew and Glen into the car and made her way to the GAA grounds. There, her elder son changed into his club colours while she and Andrew took up their places on the sidelines. It was a cold, crisp morning and, wrapped up in coats and scarves, Mary and Andrew cheered and whooped as Glen and his team romped to victory. She chatted with the other mothers and rubbed little Andrew's hands, blowing on them to warm them. They shared jokes and, as she always did, Mary bent over frequently to cuddle her little boy or smooth his hair.

After the match Mary spent time talking to the other parents about the following weekend's fixture – the team were looking forward to it, having just beaten their rivals. Then, like the other families there that day, she, Glen and Andrew went back to their car with talk of hot baths and lunch. Unlike all the other families that had lined out that day to cheer on the ten-year-old footballers, Mary, Andrew and Glen would never be seen alive again.

On the Monday morning Brian Keegan touched down at Dublin airport and took a taxi back to 39 Killakee Walk. He hoped his wife was in, as he had forgotten to bring his keys with him on his week-long trip. He was looking forward to seeing his boys, too, when they came in from school – he had a bag of gifts for them that he had picked up in the States. When he got to the house, instead of being greeted by his wife of fourteen years, he was confronted by gardaí investigating a crime scene.

Earlier, as Brian had flown across the Atlantic to the home he loved, relatives of Mary were worried: she hadn't answered calls over the weekend. Her father had rung several times and, concerned that something had happened to his daughter, he and a cousin, Liz Stubbins, had gone to the house. When there was no answer at the door, Liz, a nurse, had bent down to look through the letterbox. She was greeted by a smell so unpleasant that she almost keeled over. In the hall she could see bloody footprints. Later she said, 'I knew something bad had happened because I could smell the blood. It smelt like an operating theatre.' **GALWAY COUNTY LIBRARIES**

Liz and John knocked frantically on the door of a house nearby, where Declan Whelan lived. The off-duty garda went round to the back garden at Brian and Mary's home and peered through the kitchen window. He saw three bloodied bodies. He knew straight away that he was dealing with a crime scene and that it was vital not to touch anything that might eventually help to catch whatever crazed killer had broken into the house and killed his neighbours.

When officers arrived, they had to break into the house and immediately noted that all the doors had been bolted from inside. In the kitchen they found a bloodbath. The worktops, presses and doors were covered with bloody handprints. The boys' mutilated bodies were on the floor, their mother beside them, her neck and wrists slashed. Carving knives, covered with blood, were scattered about the scene.

The bodies were in rigor mortis and the victims had clearly been dead for at least twenty-four hours. It was hard for the investigators to grasp, but they knew that the only real explanation for what lay before their eyes was that Mary had brutally attacked her little boys before turning a knife on herself. From the handprints and the streaks of blood on the walls and presses, it was also evident that there had been a struggle and that the boys had tried to run away from their mother, grabbing at presses and worktops as they fought for their lives.

As relatives arrived, Brian Keegan was driven away. Later it was described as a mercy that he hadn't witnessed the scenes in his home. On the Wednesday he gave a statement to gardaí, saying he had no idea why his wife had done what she had. That day, postmortem examinations were completed on Mary, Glen and Andrew. The boys had suffered multiple stab wounds to their backs, faces and necks and their mother had slowly bled to death after stabbing herself and cutting her wrists.

Across the country, there was shock as early news reports focused on the horrible scenes at the house in Firhouse, where gardaí were not looking for anyone else in connection with the deaths. Closer to home, there was utter disbelief. Neighbours spoke of a contented, happy mother, who was devoted to her two young boys and had given absolutely no indication that anything was wrong or that she was suffering from any kind of mental illness. Friends talked of her kindness – Mary had been thoughtful, helpful: she would have done anything for anyone.

Investigators struggled to find any motive for her actions. The family had no financial problems, Mary had no history of depression, and there had been no sign that anything was wrong in the days leading up to the triple tragedy. Everyone was preoccupied with the terrible deaths the two little boys had suffered at the hands of their mother. They would have known exactly what was happening and pleaded with her to stop. No one could imagine what had gone through her mind when she raised a knife to the little faces she had so often tenderly wiped clean, kissed and caressed.

The following Saturday, thousands turned out to the Church of the Holy Spirit in Ballyroan as a show of sympathy to Brian, and to Mary's extended family. It was the same church where the couple had taken their marriage vows. It was left to family friend Father Howard to try to make sense of the three coffins that stood at the altar. He described Mary as a bubbly woman and a loving wife, who had fostered the talents and skills of her two young boys. He urged mourners to focus on forgiveness, and the good moments in the life of the family that had been so tragically wiped away. 'There was a bleak, dark moment in Firhouse last Saturday, a bleak, dark moment in the life of Mary, in the life of Glen, in the life of Andrew. But it was only one moment – there were billions of happy moments, of bright moments, of joyful moments, and those are the ones that we should remember,' he said.

Children from Glen and Andrew's schools, Scoil Carmel and Scoil Treasa, formed a guard of honour outside the church, along with members of Glen's GAA club. Surrounded by wreaths and red roses, Mary and her boys were buried together at nearby Bohernabreena Cemetery.

Weeks after the tragedy, as gardaí continued their investigations for the coroner's court and a nation waited to discover what had driven Mary to kill her sons, her father broke his silence to end growing speculation that his daughter had been suffering from a deep depression that she had hidden from friends and neighbours. John Flynn said that nothing could ever explain why Mary had killed herself and her children; he believed she must have 'flipped': 'Mary was the world's best. She was a great mother and she would not even let anyone breathe over those children. That's why all this is such a shock to us. But she was not depressed around the time that this happened, and she had never received any treatment for depression . . . On the Friday night before the tragedy, Mary was up here at our house with her two boys and she was in great form. The next morning she was out cheering while Glen played for his team. He was a great young fellow, really talented at sports . . . As a family we still feel very, very low. There is no getting over such a huge tragedy.'

The following October an inquest heard how Mary had inflicted fatal stab wounds to the throat and chest of both boys, then cut her own throat and punctured her lung with carving knives. One of the boys had twenty wounds. Finally, there was some sort of an explanation for what she had done. Dublin County Coroner's Court heard that Mrs Keegan had committed the killings because she was under the delusion that she was living in poverty and wanted to spare her children a life of hardship.

A professor of psychiatry, Henry Kennedy, had reviewed Mary's medical records and interviewed her family and friends. He told the court that he believed she had indeed fallen into a deep depression in the weeks before the killings and had managed to keep it secret from those around her. 'Mary Keegan was under the delusion that she was impoverished and that the children would suffer the effects of this poverty for the rest of their lives . . . I believe she did know the nature and the quality of the action in a literal sense but, because of the delusions and abnormal thoughts, she was unable to reason about the act or its consequences.' The professor also stated that, under current laws, had Mary survived her suicide attempt, she would have been declared insane.

After the inquest Brian Keegan issued a statement about his wife and their children: 'There is no anger in my heart towards her. Her actions were borne out of a will to protect our children from a harshness she perceived in this world, however inconceivable or incomprehensible this may appear to us. I would like to state clearly that I am proud to have known Mary.

She was the most loving and generous person I have ever met and she was an inspiration to me and our beautiful children, Glen and Andrew.'

A month later, as his words were still echoing in the conscience of the nation, it would be the turn of another father to acknowledge that the wife he had once known had been overtaken by a moment of madness that had changed his life for good.

To the outside world, Dr Lynn Gibbs, a psychiatrist, was living the dream. She was married to Gerard, a well-respected lecturer in aviation electronics, and they had two high-achieving children and lived in a huge gated home in Killure, Kilkenny. The couple had met as teenagers in their childhood homes in Ballypatrick, close to Carrick-on-Suir in Tipperary, where they were raised by well-to-do families.

While Gerard's upbringing was loving and stable, Lynn's was somewhat different. Her home was a large two-storey stone house at the end of a country lane. While it was well known that her mother, Iris, suffered from depression, it was 'never discussed' in the close-knit rural community. When Lynn was just seventeen, life as she knew it came to an abrupt end: her mother poisoned herself after drinking weedkiller. It was a shocking death and stunned people in an Ireland that didn't speak of such things.

Lynn reacted to her mother's suicide by developing an eating disorder, but she successfully applied to study medicine and surgery at Trinity and tried to keep her illness under wraps. In the first year she lived in supervised lodgings, but in the second, she rented a nice apartment in Dublin city centre. There, aged twenty, she had her first serious episode of clinical depression and attempted to take her own life with a drug overdose. She took a year to recover but returned to college and graduated in 1986. She went on to study psychiatry.

When she married Gerard, they decided that, to minimise work stress, she wouldn't set up her own practice and she got a job as a locum. The couple were delighted when their children came along: Ciara in 1990 and then Gearoid in 1992. But Lynn's old demons were rarely far away. She was always worried about her weight and appearance, and constantly asked her husband for reassurance. She insisted that she would never keep a set of scales in the house, but somehow managed to keep a lid on her problems as she juggled work and rearing two young children.

She was a good mother, if slightly over-protective of her daughter and son. She wanted the best for them and encouraged them to excel wherever their talents lay. Ciara, in particular, was highly academic, one of the best students at Loreto Convent in Kilkenny. She was a brilliant artist but also a born mathematician: she had been picked by the Department of Education from thousands of teenagers to take part in trials for the International Mathematics Olympiad in Vietnam the following July. A transition-year pupil, her Junior Cert results are still the stuff of legend at the school. She had been awarded ten A grades.

Two years before the tragedy, the couple had decided to build the home of their dreams – the best that money could buy – in a quieter area of Kilkenny. They installed underfloor heating, en-suite bathrooms off the generous bedrooms and fitted the sprawling red-brick mansion with high-tech electric gates that were the envy of the community. But behind the pricey gates, things were starting to unravel for Lynn, who was nearing the age at which her own mother had spiralled into a final bout of chronic depression.

During the summer of 2006, Ciara went to France. When the tall, athletic and talented sixteen-year-old returned, she had lost some weight. It quickly became apparent to her mother that she had developed anorexia. Lynn began to obsess about Ciara's eating, monitoring every morsel she swallowed and insisting she see a specialist at St Patrick's Hospital. She herself began to suffer with sleepless nights and started losing weight. Her family and friends became concerned, as she went into a depression that seemed to focus solely on her daughter. Ciara, for her part, rebelled against her mother's over-the-top concerns and had regular screaming arguments with her about visiting doctors. Lynn consulted a number of doctors she knew and was prescribed medication for depression. She told one that she had thoughts about death but had no intention of harming herself.

On Saturday, 25 November 2006, Lynn and Ciara travelled to Dublin together for a day out – Gerard and Gearoid had decided to spend the weekend in Tipperary so that mother and daughter had time to bond. In Dublin they spent the first half of the day at a UCD maths lecture for gifted students. Before they returned home, they did some shopping on Grafton Street and Ciara texted her father to say she hadn't found a suitable coat to buy her mum for Christmas.

When they got home, Lynn's friend, consultant psychiatrist Dr Marese Cheasty, visited. Over several weeks, Lynn had told her that the thought of death had come into her mind from 'time to time', but that she would never do anything about it. The two psychiatrists chatted, and late in the evening Marese bade her friend farewell, leaving her to head for bed. Some time over the following few hours, Lynn Gibb's mind snapped.

When Gerard returned to the house on the Monday morning he faced the moment that, as he would later describe it, his life fell apart. Nothing could have prepared him for the sight of his sixteen-year-old daughter lying dead on the bathroom floor as his wife Lynn slipped in and out of consciousness in a nearby bedroom. A kitchen cleaver lay nearby and the floor was covered with blood. Pills lay around Lynn and it was evident that she had overdosed. Somehow Gerard managed to summon help and Lynn was taken to St Luke's Hospital in Kilkenny and from there to St Patrick's in Dublin. She was eventually transferred to the Central Mental Hospital in Dundrum, where she would remain until her trial for the murder of her daughter.

In the meantime it was up to Gerard and thirteen-year-old Gearoid to lead mourners at St John the Baptist Church in Bally-patrick, Tipperary. Schoolfriends from Loreto Convent had made pink-covered pamphlets and handed them out to the congregation. On the front they described Ciara as 'a rainbow'. The school chaplain, Father Roderick Whearty, was left to comfort the family, while gardaí waited to interview her mother.

On 23 December, when she was finally deemed fit enough to answer their questions, Lynn made a number of admissions in a statement. She said she had difficulty in remembering most of what had happened, but she did recall that after a friend had left at eleven thirty the previous evening, she and Ciara had got ready for bed. She said she had run a bath and called Ciara into her room. 'I recall pushing her underneath the water. It was at the part where the taps were,' she told detectives. She didn't think there was a struggle but she remembered taking her daughter out of the bath and was sure she was dead. In the bedroom she said she had swallowed a mixture of sleeping tablets and anti-depressants, then got into the bath herself. She remembered not being able to stay under the water. She told detectives she couldn't recall having a knife. 'She [Ciara] was suffering from anorexia nervosa since the summer. I felt her outlook was very poor,' she added.

A few months later, she told detectives that she could remember being upstairs with Ciara but no details of her own suicide attempt. She had no recollection of taking an overdose, or having the knife, but she did remember she kept it in a block in a cupboard downstairs. Her poor memory, she said, might be the result of electroconvulsive therapy.

During her trial, consultant psychiatrists for the defence and prosecution concluded that Lynn had actually believed that by killing Ciara, she was helping her daughter escape a hopeless life ruled by anorexia. They said she had been absolutely powerless to stop herself carrying out the act. Dr Cleo van Velsen, a renowned London psychiatrist, said that in the months leading up to the tragedy, Lynn had become 'pathologically identified' with her daughter and had found it difficult to see where she left off and her daughter began.

Lynn's younger sister, Kathleen Deely, told the court that she had noticed a difference in her sister for about two months before the murder. She had lost weight, was not sleeping, and was extremely preoccupied with Ciara's weight loss. Her stepmother, Anna Hutchinson, said that the family were so concerned about Lynn that they had planned to meet on 26 November – the day Gerard had found his daughter dead. 'She was getting thinner by the day and I felt I could see she had less energy as the days went by. She seemed to be always under pressure.'

Dr Marese Cheasty had been the last person to see Lynn before the killing. She said her friend had become distressed about Ciara: 'She talked about the terrible prognosis for anorexia and how she felt Ciara would never have a career or family because of it.'

Dr Lynn Gibbs was found not guilty of murder, cleared by reason of insanity. As her trial concluded, her husband embraced her. She nodded and whispered, "It's all over."

She will remain at the Central Mental Hospital until an order is made by the State for her to be released, if she is ever deemed well enough to re-enter society.

In the very recent past, another mother ended her life before she could have a chance to taste freedom again. Ruth Murphy had never explained why she murdered her little boy, before she pulled two plastic bags over her head in the bathroom of her prison cell and slowly suffocated herself to death.

Her body was found last August in the shower cubicle of her cell in the Dóchas Centre at Mountjoy Prison in Dublin where she was serving a life sentence for drowning her seven-year-old son on a Wicklow beach nine years before. Gardaí and the Irish Prison Service launched separate inquiries into her death while she was in the care of the State, but few will need to look far for a motive.

It was June 2001, the hottest night of the year. Ruth had called to see her only son Karl: she was separated from her husband, John, after years of a difficult marriage hampered by her chronic alcoholism. By the time the relationship crumbled, Ruth's drinking was so bad that John had had her barred from the family home and had been forced to visit Karl's teachers to talk to them about his problems. After the break-up, Ruth failed to get custody of the child, who continued to live with his father. She was allowed access to her son but only under supervision. Despite the difficulties with his mother, Karl thrived and did well at school. He had a loving and secure home with his father – but Ruth harboured a terrible jealousy against her former husband and his relationship with their child.

When she called to see Karl on 22 June, at the home of a couple who were minding him for the night, she waited until their backs were turned, then bundled her little boy into her car and headed for the N11 towards Greystones. There, on the North Beach, she sat with him and they had a picnic of Coca-Cola and sandwiches, which she had bought in a local shop. They were spotted walking around the cliffs.

In the meantime, within half an hour of his estranged wife's disappearance with their son, John Murphy had reported to gardaí that Karl was missing. Shortly after ten thirty that night a scout leader rang gardaí and said he had found the body of a little boy on the North Beach. Officers arrived at the scene and soon discovered Ruth Murphy in a cave near Karl's body. She was 'incoherent' and her clothes were wet. A postmortem carried out by the then State Pathologist, John Harbison, found that the child had been forcibly drowned: there were large finger-sized bruises on his back and shoulders. It was deemed that he had put up a struggle for his life, as his mother used all her strength to keep him under the water.

Three years later, when Ruth Murphy was due to stand trial for the murder, it was expected that she would be certified insane by the psychiatrists who had treated her at the Central Mental Hospital since the time of the drowning. But as her trial was due to begin, she pleaded guilty to murder and it became apparent that the opinion of the psychiatrists was that she had not been legally insane when she had forced her only child's head under the water.

Due to her plea, scant evidence emerged at the brief hearing, before she was sentenced to the mandatory life term in prison. But it became apparent that she had a lot of drink taken when she killed her child. Tests showed she had 123 milligrams of alcohol to 100 millilitres of blood in her system, as well as traces of the tranquilliser Librium.

It also emerged that, during questioning, she had repeatedly told gardaí that Karl had accidentally drowned. Her insistence that his death had been an accident had forced officers to carry out surveys of the current and the tides on the night. But the bruising on Karl's back, shoulders and neck was damning evidence against her.

As she was transferred to Mountjoy Prison, Ruth Murphy was placed on suicide watch, but she settled in well to prison life, even befriending Catherine Nevin, another notorious killer, who has been locked up since 2000 for murdering her husband Tom four years previously at their pub, Jack White's Inn near Arklow, in County Wicklow. Prison sources regularly described Ruth as 'a troubled soul', who was quiet and withdrawn. In the six years that followed her conviction, she was granted temporary release every month, due to her good behaviour, to visit her son's grave. She had last been to the little plot at Killoughter Cemetery in Ashford two weeks before she took her own life. She left no suicide note.

Ruth Murphy never told anyone why she had killed her little boy, but those who investigated her case believe it was a misguided act of revenge against her husband, fuelled by alcohol and depression. It will never be known if she planned to take so long to join Karl: had she lost her nerve to kill herself after she had cut his life so tragically short on that warm summer evening?

6

THEY HAD IT ALL
The Flood Tragedy

Lorraine Kehoe was a local beauty in the rural parish of Clonroche in County Wexford, where she had grown up. She had chiselled features, blonde hair, blue eyes, and was a member of a famed local sporting family. The second youngest child of Jim and Kathleen Kehoe, she was doted on by siblings Seamus, Martina, Rosemarie, David, Derek and Peter. Her father had hailed from a family of seventeen, whose skills at hurling and camogie were legendary in the townlands around Clonroche. His own father had been a prominent player during the 1930s and 1940s and had instilled a deep love of the games in his large family.

Lorraine's aunts had even outshone her uncles, making their way to All-Ireland level as young camogie players: Gretta had captained the Wexford team in 1975 while Brigid had won medals three times between 1968 and 1975. Other aunts had shone on the pitch, too – Bernie, Annie and Josephine – while uncles John, Tommy and Davy had all starred at county level in hurling. From a young age Lorraine had spent her weekends on the sidelines, cheering on the teams and mixing with the army of cousins and other relatives who lived in close proximity to one another around the pretty countryside.

She had gone to her local national school, St Joseph's in Poulpeasty, before completing her secondary education at the Mercy Convent in nearby New Ross. From there she had joined the staff at Culleton Insurance, where she was noted for her intelligence, diligence and the life she brought to the office. But her real passion lay in sports and fitness and she had always hoped to combine her passion for working with people with a job in that area.

By her early twenties Lorraine could go nowhere without turning heads. She had a fantastic figure, a bright smile that lit up her face and dazzling eyes. She modelled part-time but had no ambition to move away from her family and make it on the catwalks in Dublin or London. She had excelled on stage throughout her teens, and was involved in local pantomimes and musicals. She was also a key member of the choir at her church, St Clement's, in Cloughbawn, where she could be seen every Sunday lining up for worship.

In 1991, at the age of twenty-two, she entered the Wexford Strawberry Festival, after much encouragement from friends, family and colleagues. The festival had been running since 1967 – three years before Lorraine was born – and was a celebration of the local crop that is an emblem of summertime throughout Ireland. Each year a beauty was chosen to be crowned the Strawberry Queen and, in recent years, the winner had been sent on to represent neighbouring Waterford in the Rose of Tralee Festival. Lorraine took to the stage and was a runaway success, wowing judges with her good looks and her musical abilities. Her extended family turned out in their droves to see her carried on a float down the Main Street in Enniscorthy, with her pink sash and sparkling crown.

Waterford were excited at their prospects in the prestigious Rose of Tralee that year and reckoned that, with Lorraine Kehoe as their representative, they could just about snatch the title. She had model good looks and was exactly the type of girl that the Rose of Tralee festival was all about. She stood out from the crowd and was bubbly, friendly and well used to appearing on stage. She also had the country innocence that tends to take the crown. All the Roses, who hailed from first-, second- and third-generation Irish families across the world and at home, were given an escort for the week-long festival, which culminated in a televised selection process. Most applicants were between twenty-one and thirty years of age, unmarried and were vetted by a committee. Those who had a boyfriend – Lorraine was one – often requested that they accompany them for the competition. For seven months she had been dating a local man. Diarmuid Flood was twenty-five, the son of a well-to-do local businessman.

The Floods, like the Kehoes, were well got around the Wexford area, and they too were associated with hurling. Diarmuid's father, Seanie, and two cousins had all lined out for their county in the 1950s. Members of his family were still mainstays of local clubs' senior teams. Neither Diarmuid nor his brothers, Robert, Tom and John, played hurling seriously into adulthood, but they had followed their father into the family business, an established and profitable water-drilling concern that Seanie had run for many years. The family lived in the centre of Clonroche in a beautiful period property and ran their business from the yards behind it. Diarmuid had attended secondary school in New Ross and had noticed

Lorraine when she was still just a schoolgirl, but he had only built up the courage to ask her out when she was twenty-one. She had accepted and they had quickly become an item.

August 1991 was exciting for the young couple, as they packed their bags and headed for Tralee for the Rose Festival. Diarmuid looked after his Rose throughout the week and mixed with the other escorts, while the girls primped and preened for the stage. On the night of the show Lorraine was a hot favourite – a number of bookies even tipped her to win. During her brief appearance on stage, she spoke about her relationship with her future husband. Host Gay Byrne remarked on her beauty and told her that her eyes were like 'two limpid pools of the Mediterranean'. She blushed and giggled, and told him she liked playing guitar, singing in the local choir and taking part in the Cloughbawn Variety Group. After pointing out Diarmuid in the audience, Gay Byrne quipped, 'So are you going to marry this fellow?' to rapturous laughter from the audience.

'Well, yes, if he asks me, I will,' Lorraine replied, to whoops and cheers. 'After seven months?' joked Gay Byrne. 'Does he know that you're going to marry him?'

Lorraine giggled again. 'No,' she said, looking coyly into the audience and then to her handsome dark-haired suitor in the front row.

Lorraine didn't win the contest – the crown went to the Cork Rose – but she returned to Wexford and, over the next few years, continued to help out at the Wexford Rose Centre where she was often asked to be a judge.

Four years after her exchange with Gay Byrne, Lorraine and Diarmuid were married and settled down to live in his family home on Clonroche Main Street, where he worked for the family business. In 1998 Diarmuid took over Sean Flood Pumps

Debbie and Greg Fox in their grocery shop, situated adjacent to the bungalow, below, where they lived. In July 2001, the murdered bodies of Debbie and her two children, Trevor (9) and Killian (7), were found.

Greg Fox being led by gardai from the courthouse where he pleaded guilty to the murders.

Family photo of Adrian Dunne with wife Ciara and daughters Léan and Shania. The family was found dead at their home in Monageer, Co. Wexford in April 2007, in what is understood to have been a murder-suicide pact between the parents. Below: Adrian's funeral in Wexford. Ciara and their children were buried some three hundred miles away in Donegal.

Devastated mother Christine O'Sullivan holds up a photo of her missing daughter Deirdre, who was abducted by her father Chris Crowley in December 1999. Chris Crowley (below), upon discovery in 2001, shot and killed his daughter before turning the gun on himself.

Nollaig Owen (left), a young mother who, in a state of severe post-natal depression, drowned herself and her baby Tadhg in the Araglin river in Cork.

On 11 February 2006, mother-of-two Mary Keegan (above) stood on the sidelines with son Andrew (left, top) to cheer on son Glen (bottom, right) in a local football match. That was the last time they were seen alive. Soon after, she violently murdered both of her children, before killing herself in their home, below, in Firhouse, Dublin.

Ruth Murphy, left, outside the court where she pleaded guilty to murdering her son Karl in 2001, after abducting him. In 2010, Ruth Murphy killed herself in Mountjoy Prison.

The Flood tragedy. Below: The burned-out remnants of the family home in Wexford, which Diarmuid Flood set alight after suffocating his children, Mark and Julie, and shooting his wife Lorraine. He then shot himself. Left: Diarmuid and Lorraine in happier times.

The Flood funeral (above). Below, a family picture of murderer Shane Clancy who, in August 2009, killed Sebastian Creane, with whose girlfriend he was obsessed, before turning the knife on himself.

Shane's grave.

Avid photographer and musician Sebastian Creane, (left) was just 22 years old when he was stabbed to death by Shane Clancy at his home in Bray. Below: Mourners at his funeral, including (right) Nuala Creane, Sebastian's mother, and his girlfriend Jennifer Hannigan (left), of whom Shane Clancy believed he had been put on the earth to be with.

Tregedy at Ballycotton, Cork, November 2010. Above: The burnt out shell of John Butler's car, which he doused in petrol before crashing headlong into a wall, fatally injuring himself. The bodies of his two young daughters, Zoe and Ella, whom he had murdered, were later found in their home. Butler (right) had been a local GAA star in his day. At his funeral (below) he was described as a 'beloved husband and father'.

Ltd and, with a construction boom on the way, planned to develop it and make a fresh success of it for the future. By now Lorraine worked in the office there, but in the meantime she had trained as a fitness and yoga instructor and had begun running classes locally. She continued to sing in the choir, and helped out in local community centres and with her variety club. In 2001, the couple's first child, Mark, was born, followed quickly in 2003 by little Julie.

While Diarmuid immersed himself in his business, Lorraine looked after the children, but he was a hands-on father too, and when Mark started school at Clonroche National, he took the little boy every day to the school gate. A year later when Julie started he always walked both children there before returning to start his day at his desk.

Lorraine and Diarmuid were envied by many and were even nicknamed 'Barbie and Ken'. They seemed to have it all. While he was quiet, she was outgoing. They were glamorous and both drove a Mercedes. Their period home, with pretty ivy growing up the front, was one of the nicest houses in the locality; their children were gorgeous and showing early promise at hurling and camogie. They enjoyed foreign holidays and regularly dined out. Unlike other young couples, they had never been burdened with a mortgage and their company accounts, which would later be investigated, showed that they were on the up. Diarmuid was a good businessman. When he had taken over the company in 1998, he had decided to expand it from sinking deep wells to providing water pumps for landscaped gardens and new houses. Business was booming.

At the same time, Lorraine's fitness classes were proving to be a huge success, and with her slim frame, fresh skin and lively demeanour, she could have been no better advertisement for healthy living. Her classes were popular with local women, many of whom had children attending the same school as Lorraine's little boy and girl. She would regularly have up to thirty in a class on Tuesdays and Thursdays at the local community centre. In her spare time she drove Mark to hurling practice and Julie to her Irish dancing lessons. The family were members of a local gym and leisure centre, which they regularly attended together.

On the morning of Friday, 25 April 2008, Diarmuid was at work as usual when the office secretary arrived at nine thirty. Throughout the morning he flitted between the workshop and the office and appeared to be his usual self. Lorraine arrived into the office shortly after midday and Diarmuid remained there until he left to collect the children after school. Friday was swimming day, when he brought Mark and Julie to the Ferrycarrig Hotel, where the family held membership. Lorraine was seen at around five o'clock, running across the road to purchase something from a local shop, and the family left the pool some time after six p.m. as usual.

Just over an hour later a local man, Michael Lawless, bought a packet of painkillers from the Gala garage in Clonroche and drove slowly towards his home in his black Almera. His route took him past the Floods' house, and as he watched, he saw Diarmuid, wearing a green jumper, closing the gates at his house. It was around seven twenty-five p.m. What happened behind the walls of the Flood family home over the next ten hours has remained a mystery. It shook a community to its core.

At five thirty a.m. on Saturday, 26 April, John Kehoe was woken by a series of bangs. Initially there were one or two and then a more persistent noise, like a firecracker. He looked out of his window and saw, to his horror, flames shooting from the two-storey house owned by his neighbours, the Flood family.

John phoned the gardaí in Enniscorthy and told them to send the fire brigade immediately. Then he threw on his clothes and ran out to the burning house.

He found others there, and despite the panic that ensued, they fetched an iron bar from the yard and pushed in a downstairs window. In the meantime someone else produced a ladder and raised it to the upstairs front bedroom. John Kehoe scrambled up the rungs until he got to the windowsill above. It was nearly daylight, and as he peered in he could just make out Lorraine. She was lying on her side, on top of the bedclothes, with her face towards the window.

John broke the window and hauled himself into the room, ignoring the licking flames and the billowing black smoke below him. He called to Lorraine and reached out, shaking her leg but she didn't move. 'Get up! Get up!' he called frantically, smoke beginning to engulf his lungs, but there was a deathly silence, save for the noise of the fire. Then he saw blood on her chest. He grabbed a blanket and draped it over her body. Then he struggled to make his way on to the landing, calling for the children. He could hear no crying – nothing.

At this point the fire was aggressively spreading from the right side of the house to the left. The smoke and flames were so strong that John had trouble breathing. Outside he could hear his neighbours shouting for him to get out. He staggered back into the bedroom and somehow clambered down the ladder where he waited with the gathered crowd, hopelessly watching the flames envelop the house as the first fire engines started to arrive.

The officers immediately started to fight the blaze. It wasn't until they had the flames under control that they could enter the house. Chris Wyles was one of the first inside the smouldering building. He made his way up the stairs to discover horrific scenes. Lorraine was in her bedroom, lying on the bed and covered with the blanket that John Kehoe had thrown over her earlier. In a second bedroom the body of a little girl clutching a teddy bear was almost untouched by the flames but blackened by smoke. On what appeared to be the landing a third body, a boy's, was lying on debris. Mark was unrecognisable.

At the same time, firefighter Anthony Nolan was in what seemed to be a sitting room when he spotted a body lying back in an armchair. It was so badly burned that he couldn't tell if it was male or female.

The house had been gutted by the inferno, which had seemingly started downstairs. The noises that had woken John Kehoe had been roof tiles exploding from the intensity of the heat.

Gardaí had arrived and were cordoning off the scene to save any forensic evidence. They were also taking names and addresses of eye-witnesses, who would be interviewed in what was sure to be a lengthy investigation. Chief Superintendent John Roche knew that he was going to have to leave no stone unturned when it came to finding out what had happened to the once vibrant young family, who were now little more than a charred mass of bones. He had been informed that a shotgun had been discovered in the remains of the fire, close to where a body lay slumped in an armchair. He called in support from the Garda Technical Bureau and the State Pathologist's Office. The presence of the firearm prompted him to inform the National Bureau of Criminal Investigation.

By morning, those who came to look at the eerie, smouldering remains of the Floods' once beautiful period house could just about see the small pink clothes fluttering on the line in the garden behind. They were a stark reminder of how a life could be taken so quickly without warning. A little playhouse stood beside the line, and on the side of the house the business sign for Sean Flood Pumps was fully intact.

When a priest arrived to give the family the last rites he was told that it wasn't possible for him to enter the scene so he had to say the prayers outside.

From the outset and even before the Deputy State Pathologist, Declan Gilsenan, had completed his examination of the bodies, it was evident that this was yet another unthinkable crime. As fire and technical experts swarmed through the house, it quickly became apparent that the fire had been no ordinary domestic accident. An accelerant had been used. That was why it had become so intense so quickly. And the blood that John Kehoe had noticed on Lorraine's body was the result of a gunshot wound. She had a gaping hole in her chest, and from the way she was lying, it seemed that she had been dead before the fire was even set.

Circumstantial evidence suggested that the unidentified body in the living room was Diarmuid's, and a preliminary examination of the remains showed that he had been shot in the face at point-blank range. The team needed to await technical examinations but, again, circumstantial evidence indicated that the shotgun that lay beside the armchair was likely the weapon that had killed Lorraine and Diarmuid.

Gardaí suspected they were dealing with yet another murder-suicide. Once the ownership of the firearm was established, they could pretty much rule out the involvement of anyone else in these deaths. Up to fifty members of the force were called in to help with the inquiry while officers were dispatched to ask tough questions from a fragile community, numb with shock and grief.

Throughout the day, locals spoke in hushed tones about the

Floods, many refusing to believe the unimaginable horror that Diarmuid could have killed them all. They came and stood around the cordoned-off house and simply stared, as though the blackened embers would whisper the truth. Others busied themselves, arriving at the homes of the grief-stricken, armed with trays of sandwiches, pots of tea and fruit flans. They offered support and help with a community spirit long forgotten in many corners of a new, wealthy Ireland.

By Sunday morning, those who had been sceptical about Diarmuid's role in the tragedy were left in no doubt: headlines screamed from every newspaper about the deranged father who had been driven to kill: he appeared to have suffocated his children before blasting his wife to death – a husband who had had it all, but had thrown it away in a fit of madness. Rumours were spreading about financial difficulties the family may have been facing, and in one paper the HSE had refused to comment on speculation that Diarmuid had visited a doctor in recent weeks.

In the local church, Father Richard Hayes held a special memorial mass. In front of a packed, stunned congregation he said that while the community was united 'in sadness and sorrow, they were not without hope'. He pledged the support of the whole parish to the Flood and Kehoe families, and said that the deaths had left everyone 'numb, helpless and lost'. He had been asked by the Bishop of Ferns, Dr Denis Brennan, to pray for the families and remember them in services.

Later the bishop issued his own statement: 'I am very mindful of the family and friends of those who have died, the local parish and diocesan communities and the many who share my deep sadness at this most unfortunate tragedy. Across the nation today, thoughts and prayers are turning to Clonroche, to the parents and children who have died, and the harrowing effects on those family members, neighbours and friends who have received this dreadful news.'

The then Taoiseach, Bertie Ahern, also offered his condolences: 'It would really, I think, shake anybody's heart. We've just seemed, in the last few years, to have had a number of these tragedies and all I can do is give my deepest of sympathy to the relatives and close friends of the family. I mean, for them . . . It must just be heart- and earth-shattering for them.'

While the forensic investigations continued at the Flood home on Main Street, Wexford County Council personnel diverted traffic away from the crime scene. But despite the cordon, those who came could see for themselves the reality of what was left of a family: a desecrated home, windows broken, and a blackened hole where half of the roof was in ruins. As speculation mounted about how a father had killed his own children, the gardaí decided to hold a press conference. Garda Superintendent Kevin Donohoe, who then headed up the force's Press Office, issued a brief statement: 'All four bodies had injuries consistent with the fire – there were no other injuries of note to Julie and Mark. There were some injuries on Diarmuid and Lorraine, which have yet to be determined,' he said. While the injuries might not have been determined, they were so substantial that when Sergeant Brendan Moore brought Lorraine's brother Seamus and Diarmuid's brother John to Dublin to identify the bodies, it was deemed inappropriate, considering the condition they were in. It was decided that DNA would be used to identify the children, and dental records for their parents.

The body believed to be Diarmuid Flood's was in a particularly bad way. The upper part of the head had been blown off so violently by the shotgun blast that pieces of skull and brain matter had been discovered in the debris of the house. On top of that, it was horrifically burned. The child's body, discovered on what had been thought initially was an upstairs landing, was unidentifiable. Lorraine's body had been blackened by smoke and damaged by fire – and, of course, there was the wound in her chest.

Newspaper reporters scoured the village, and the *Irish Mirror*'s correspondent came across Jim Redmond. 'I was woken by the noise at about five thirty a.m. The slate tiles on the roof were exploding. It sounded like fireworks. When I got outside the entire house was ablaze. There was nothing anybody could do. The roof was already collapsing. Two men from the estate burst down the door and tried to make their way up the stairs. But they were forced back by the heat and the smoke. We were just standing there in shock. The Floods were the finest family you could ever meet. They were great people. Diarmuid was always helping people out,' he said.

Lorraine's uncle, Denis Kennedy, a local councillor, was nominated to speak on behalf of the family. He said that neither side knew what had triggered Diarmuid's actions: 'They were a model family and a gorgeous couple. There was no issue that we are aware of. Maybe in the fullness of time something will be discovered.' Diarmuid's and Lorraine's parents would never get over the shock, he added. 'We are a tight-knit community, and all we can hope is that this community spirit and people's prayers can get us through it.' From that first statement, it was apparent that the Flood and Kehoe families were in this together.

By Monday morning, parents of pupils at Clonroche National School were trying to explain to their small children what had happened to their friends Julie and Mark, and why they would no longer be attending the little school. That

Monday the children made their way past the garda barriers at the burned-out home of their classmates. The road was still closed, so parents had to park their cars further down the village and walk the last stretch. Many gathered at the gates for a spontaneous moment of silence before they brought their children to their classrooms. Most held the little hands tighter, hugged them a little longer and walked away a little more reluctantly than they had before.

A prayer service was held at the school, before Principal Norma Doyle read a press statement to the waiting media, complimenting the youngsters on their bravery: 'I would like to take this opportunity to extend my deepest sympathies to both families at this terrible time. We are all devastated and deeply saddened by the events of the past two days. This is a very close-knit community and we are trying to come to terms with this terrible tragedy. Our school has lost two beautiful students, Julie in Junior Infants and Mark in Senior Infants. They were happy, loving children and we will miss them terribly.' She said the school was instigating its critical-incident plan, with psychologists available to offer advice and support to the 120 children.

At the same time, the Flood and Kehoe families showed another sign of unity, this time issuing a joint statement through Denis Kennedy: 'Our two families, so well known and loved by each other, must now begin the process of rebuilding our lives following this tragedy. There was a mass in Lorraine's parents' home, attended by all the Flood family, the Kehoe family and friends and neighbours. They are all shattered but they are supporting and comforting each other. In the light of recent events, with much sorrow in our hearts, we the bereaved families ask to be afforded the privacy to mourn and cherish our dearly departed. We ask the media to understand our wishes to be allowed the dignity to put to rest our loved ones without undue media attention and speculation. We hope that in the fullness of time we may all learn to understand what could have led to this tragic occurrence. We urge the media, our wider community and the nation to understand how deeply we have been affected by this tragedy and to realise that Diarmuid and Lorraine were children to their parents, siblings to their siblings. Mark and Julie were grandchildren to their grand-parents, and loved by all who knew them. Our two families, so well known to each other, must now begin the process of rebuilding our lives shattered by this tragedy. To all those who offered condolences and support at this time, we are eternally grateful. May Mark, Julie, Diarmuid and Lorraine rest in peace.' The statement added that the funeral arrangements would be made in the coming days and that the family would be buried together in Cloughbawn Cemetery following mass at St Clement's Church.

The show of togetherness and solidarity was in stark contrast to what had happened when Adrian Dunne had smothered his children, strangled his wife and hanged himself. On that occasion he was shunned, and separated in death from those he had chosen to be with forever. Somehow the Floods and the Kehoes would do things differently.

As the days wore on and an intensive garda investigation got under way, it proved extremely difficult for officers to find anything in the background of the Flood family that could explain Diarmuid's actions early that Saturday morning. While newspapers speculated that he had run into financial difficulty and had been suffering from depression, officers were baffled. Whatever had happened, there was no suggestion of a chronic dysfunction in the mind of the businessman, and there was no evidence of excessive drinking, debt or infidelity. Officers knew some story lay behind what had occurred that night, but as they poured all their resources into it, they simply couldn't find out what it was. But they were convinced that somebody knew something.

The hard evidence they had gathered proved that Diarmuid was planning for the future. He had ordered supplies for his business and booked a family holiday. Also in the recent past, he had secured shotgun cartridges and bought petrol.

The case remained on the front pages of the papers for days, and locals described Diarmuid as a 'pleasant, successful family man', who was 'devoted to his children and his business'. Lorraine was spoken of as a beautiful, stylish, sociable person and a dedicated mother who adored her children. There were reports of a phone call Diarmuid was supposed to have made at five a.m. prior to the blaze, and much was made of how young Mark had been discovered: had he woken and made his way on to the landing as his home turned into a raging inferno? With the family looking for answers and a media frenzy, the gardaí decided to hold a second and more detailed press briefing.

Superintendent Kevin Donohue addressed a large crowd of media. He revealed that officers were investigating the possibility that the children had been drugged before the house was set on fire. He said there was no evidence of physical trauma on either of their bodies and that investigators were now waiting for toxicology results on their blood samples. He also confirmed that used and unused ammunition had been found in the house and that the fire had possibly been fuelled. Contrary to earlier reports, he said that Mark had been discovered in his room and that his and his father's body were badly charred, unlike Julie's and Lorraine's.

Donohue went on: 'Gardaí have interviewed a huge number

of people at this stage and we will continue to do that over the next few days. We are slowly acquiring information which will help piece together what transpired in the house on Saturday morning. Gardaí are liaising with any agencies, bodies or individuals who we feel can assist.' He said that the family had made plans for that weekend and the following days and confirmed that no suicide note had been found in the ruins of their home. 'We are now satisfied that Mark actually was in a bedroom. The wall, a stud partition dividing the landing from the bedroom, was actually destroyed by the fire so the initial visual examination indicated he was on the landing. He wasn't on the landing: he was in a bedroom on the remnant of a bed.'

Phone records were being examined and no relative had received a call from Diarmuid early that morning.

The superintendent would not confirm whether or not Diarmuid had attended a doctor: 'You can go down a certain line and things are looking like they fit and something comes to the fore that throws that out the window.' His off-the-cuff remark gave an indication of the frustration that investigators felt. They were baffled. Diarmuid Flood had purchased shotgun cartridges a fortnight before the tragedy but he had also made arrangements to have his car serviced, booked the family holiday – and had made an appointment for psychiatric assessment, although this would not emerge until the inquest. He had visited a local GP more than once in the days leading up to the tragedy. Financially he was sound: in the previous year the family had lived off a little over €100,000 but they had no mortgage and they ran their cars through the company. In 2005, the directors had told the Companies Registration Office that they made almost €68,000; in 2006 that had risen to just over €73,000. The accounts showed that the company had no major assets or debts. While business had slowed somewhat in the past year, the Floods seemed to have had little to worry about.

In the run-up to the funerals, shock gave way to anger. Locals vented their fury at a man who could kill two young children and his wife. Some spoke of Diarmuid as a controlling husband who rarely let his wife out of his sight. Others said he was so terrified of losing her that he had become obsessive. 'She was his prized possession,' one unnamed local told a newspaper. 'She couldn't have a life outside the marriage. He wouldn't have let her out of his sight when they were out together. He was completely devoted but that devotion had turned to obsession.' As funeral arrangements were finalised, investigating officers were questioning a local doctor and were gaining some idea of Diarmuid's mental state shortly before the tragedy.

On 1 May, a bright and sunny day, the remains of Julie, Mark, Lorraine and Diarmuid were removed to the church where Lorraine had sung in the choir and attended Sunday mass since she was a little girl. It was an incredible sight for the throng waiting along the way to pay their respects: on the crest of a hill on the rural road that led to the church, a huge cortège of at least five hundred family members and friends came into view, followed by the two hearses. A sister of Diarmuid's clutched a framed photograph of beauty queen Lorraine on the day she was crowned at the Strawberry Fair. The Kehoes and Floods comforted one another as the giant procession snaked its way down the hill. The anguish of Clonroche had been building for a week, and as relatives lifted the two little white coffins from the hearses, nothing was heard except a mass intake of breath and birdsong.

Local people had set up overflow car parks and arranged the flowers at the 150-year-old church where generations of the two families had worshipped. Two enormous cards waited inside, signed by children at the school: Julie's was a brightly coloured collage of butterflies and flowers, Mark's a jumble of boyish dreams – trains, cars and planes.

Father Richard Hayes broke the silence: 'Now we feel lost, helpless and frightened. Most likely we are angry and we want to blame somebody, but this is not the time to reduce the God of Jesus to our own size. Yes, it is a terrible tragedy but God is much greater if we can care, love and try to comfort . . . We all come across things in life that are sad – very sad – but this is one which is almost impossible to comprehend. We also keep in mind that this is a very painful tragedy that involves the loss of small children, Mark and Julie, and their parents Diarmuid and Lorraine. Let us be sensitive and caring to the bereaved families as we consider the rawness of their great loss, their vulnerability, their darkness and their pain.'

At the altar, two oak coffins were flanked by two little white ones. All four bore photographs. The three of Julie showed her skipping, playing with the family dog, and wrapped in her winter woollies; Mark was grinning mischievously, and Lorraine was cradling her children. On Diarmuid's coffin there was just one picture: of him and his wife on their wedding day. The school choir sang Lorraine's favourite tune, 'A Little Peace', which she herself had performed at the Rose of Tralee festival.

It was as though all the sorrows of the world had been distilled into the tiny churchyard. Around that graveyard were hundreds of family and friends, members of a tightly bonded community, with no answers – with nothing but questions.

A year had passed before anyone could make sense of Diarmuid Flood's actions at his home in Wexford that night. At the inquest, toxicology results were released, which showed that Mark and Julie had been given no sedatives on the night of their murder. While it was impossible to say exactly how they died, Pathologist Declan Gilsenan said his best guess was that the children had been smothered by a pillow because there was no evidence of smoke inhalation in their lungs: this confirmed that they were dead before the fire was started. The toxicology results also showed traces of anti-depressant in Lorraine's system but the coroner for North Wexford, Dr Sean Nixon, said that she had been in good health and spirits, and that there was no suggestion she had been depressed.

However, Diarmuid had had 'serious mental health issues', which he had managed to keep hidden from his family and friends. A doctor and nurse from Clonroche Medical Centre said he had visited them on a number of occasions leading up to that weekend. Dr James Kirrane said Diarmuid had visited the surgery on Thursday, 17 April, a week before the tragedy, and complained that he was depressed because work was quiet and he had felt low during the winter. He had told his doctor that he was waking up in the middle of the night, sweating and with heart palpitations. The doctor had broached the subject of self-harm and suicide, but Diarmuid had said he would never consider taking any such actions. However, he did fear he had cancer. Following a full physical examination, he was told he was in good health – but he had continued to insist that something was wrong with him.

Diarmuid Flood had been his patient for a number of years, Kirrane said, and while he had felt depressed, his main complaints were physical. He had mentioned aching in his groin, but examination had shown nothing abnormal in the area. Dr Kirrane said he had written to St Senan's Hospital in Enniscorthy to request an appointment for Mr Flood to meet a psychiatrist to discuss his low moods and anxiety. An appointment was made for 28 April – two days after the tragedy – but even so, Kirrane saw his patient again: he was still complaining of an aching groin and also back pain. He told his doctor he wanted a colonoscopy, but Kirrane preferred to wait for the outcome of the psychiatric consultation at St Senan's.

Nurse Elaine McCarthy said that Diarmuid was very conscious of his health and that he was desperate to keep any problems to himself: 'He wouldn't wait at the centre if there were other people present. On Monday morning, before he died, he came in at nine twenty but left until the coast was clear. He returned at ten thirty,' she said. She had taken a blood sample, labelled it 'Urgent' and filled in the necessary paperwork so he could take it to St John's Hospital. On the Friday, less than twenty-four hours before he was found dead, he attended the surgery again, wanting to know if the results of the tests were back. They were not.

At eleven fifteen the nurse contacted him to tell him the results were good and that his cholesterol, which had earlier been a little high, was back to normal. Later in the day Diarmuid Flood arrived to check the results for himself. 'He was in the prime of his health but he remained worried, mentioning his mother's cancer and the possibility that it could be passed on. He didn't want to see the locum doctor on duty but made an appointment for Dr Kirrane on 28 April.'

Dr Nixon ruled that Diarmuid was suffering from a depressive illness, had kept it to himself and had worked as normal up to the day that he died. He said his mind had been very disturbed and he had had serious concerns about his health. 'What happened, I cannot explain, maybe no one can explain in cases of familicide. Strangely, this may have been seen as an act of love by Diarmuid Flood. This has been a very, very hard year for the Flood and Kehoe families. I know the inquest will not bring all the answers. In cases like this, there are no winners, only victims. Mr Flood loved his wife and children and was very close to them. The family had no relationship problems and no financial worries at the time.'

Like Mary Keegan, who butchered her two young sons and herself, illogically believing them to be stuck in a poverty trap, he had hidden his deepest fears from those who knew him best. Like Lynn Gibbs, who murdered her teenage daughter believing she was saving her from the harsh world of anorexia, Diarmuid Flood appears to have become so obsessed with his health that he could see nothing ahead but pain and suffering, and had developed such a warped view of the world around him that he chose to get out. Why he couldn't have gone alone is anyone's guess.

7

BORN TO BE WITH YOU
The Case of Shane Clancy

'Shane said I was put on this planet to be with him and no one was ever going to love me as much as him.'
Jennifer Hannigan

Dunnes Stores in Cornelscourt, South Dublin, is a quiet, deserted place in the early hours of the morning, populated with staff stacking shelves, shift workers in for their groceries and the odd new parent looking for refuge from a crying baby. It is a huge store, a flagship for the cut-price chain where generations of Southsiders have purchased pretty much anything from a garden chair to a litre of strawberry-flavoured milk. Half of the store contains aisles of groceries and the other, a mish-mash of clothing, accessories and hardware. It is the epitome of modern-day consumerism, open 24/7. And it was exactly the spot where Shane Clancy knew he could get what he needed in the early hours of an August morning. The tall, handsome student had just one thing on his mind when he left his Skoda in the giant car park outside Dunnes on 16 August 2009, and purposefully strode past the CCTV cameras. For four months Shane Clancy had just one girl on his mind and now he wanted her more than ever. But, first, he needed a knife.

Like the countless other young men and women home from their summer travels and preparing to head back to college within a matter of weeks, Clancy had been out that night. But unlike his contemporaries, who were either safely tucked up in their beds or enjoying the flirtatious early days of new romance, he had somewhere to go and something very important to do. It was after four a.m. when he made his way to the household section and chose a block of discount knives, handed over five euro to an assistant and made his way back to his car.

Pulling out of the car park, he turned left on to the N11, heading out of town. But instead of turning off the road towards Dalkey, where he rented a little bedsit, he continued on towards Bray and back to the house where he had recently dropped off a young man.

For those who knew Shane Clancy, he was bright and hard-working, a gentle soul. That person was unrecognisable from the young man who now drove to Bray with his block of knives on the passenger seat beside him. He was no longer the man who gave away his train fare to a beggar and instead walked the seven miles home from Trinity College; he was no longer the joker who loved to make his little brothers and sisters laugh; and he was no longer the gentle giant who lived life to the full. That night, Clancy was a hunter, and he was in an unstoppable, murderous rage.

Shane Clancy was born in Dublin and grew up with his parents, Leonie Fennell and Patrick Clancy, in the working-class suburb of Ballybrack. The pair had three children together, Shane, Liam and Jake. They split when the boys were still young. Leonie, a hairdresser, worked hard to give her boys everything they wanted and needed, and instilled in them the importance of education. Eventually she met and fell in love with Tony Donnelly, and the pair went on to marry and have four children together. They decided to rear their brood in a rural environment away from the rougher elements of Ballybrack, Dun Laoghaire and Sallynoggin.

The new family home was a lovely bungalow with a large garden in Wicklow, just outside the little village of Redcross, where their children were enrolled in local schools. Shane got on well with his stepfather but while he was studying for his Leaving Certificate, aged just seventeen, he moved out of his home to be nearer the city and his friends. It was a big decision for such a young teenager, but his family accepted it as he had always seemed so much older than his years. His parents certainly had no worries that he would go wild.

Shane didn't drink, he loved to keep fit and he was adamant that he was going to college. He chose to live in Dalkey, a village famous for its celebrity residents and large houses but equally populated with rental accommodation. His bedsit was in an old period house just across the road from one of the town's busiest bars, the Club: to fund it and his subsequent college fees, Shane took a job there as a barman. Dalkey was a busy town so there was no shortage of work for him, and because he lived just across the road, he was often called in to do extra hours or shifts if things got busy at the bar. He made a healthy living that allowed him to run a small car while he was still a student. His father and other relatives lived nearby.

In fact, his family were well-known in the village as they had long had a little fleet of boats down at Coliemore Harbour, which ferried tourists and visitors to and from Dalkey Island.

Shane finished school with excellent results and secured a place at Trinity College, Dublin, where he enrolled for a degree in Irish and theology. He had always been a deep thinker and immersed himself in his course and a variety of societies at the college. He was teetotal, but he still enjoyed the college social life and would often be the last man standing on a night out. His life was simple: he worked hard at college and at his job. He visited his father, Patrick, a few times a week at his home in nearby Dun Laoghaire and regularly had dinner with him. At weekends he drove to Redcross to stay with his mother and bring his brothers and sisters for fast-food and to the beach.

Two years after he moved to Dalkey, he was introduced to a local girl. She had caught his eye from the minute he had first seen her. Jennifer Hannigan was fresh out of school, a pretty blonde girl who, at eighteen, had secured a place at a nearby art college. She came from a middle-class family and had grown up in the Ballinclea Heights estate located on the side of Killiney Hill, which overlooks Dalkey and its surrounding bay. She had attended the fee-paying Loreto School in the village, where she had excelled academically. She couldn't help but notice Shane when she was introduced to him by her friend, who knew him because they took the DART into Trinity College together. He was well over six foot tall and, with his strong good looks, it was hard to resist when he asked her out.

The couple had a few dates and eventually started going out regularly in the first few days of 2006. Shane introduced her to the Club's owner, Seamus Shearon, who agreed to take her on as a lounge girl so she could make some pocket money. Jennifer was living at home so wasn't under the same financial pressures as Shane, but she took to the job like a duck to water and, with her chatty personality, became a hit with staff and customers alike. She earned good tips, which came in handy on nights out with her friends at the Dun Laoghaire Institute of Art, Design and Technology. At work Shane was quiet and some remarked that he appeared to brood. He often said little when he stood behind the bar but he was reliable, a hard worker and good at the job.

At the start of their relationship, Jennifer and Shane were like any teenage couple in the throes of an early romance. While he was besotted with her, she was equally enthralled by him. They went for long walks, enjoyed trips to the cinema and went to pubs, even though Shane didn't drink. Jennifer had a wide circle of friends with whom she had grown up around Dalkey, but he didn't have the same background, so had to rely on her to include him in conversations when they were in company. As they attended different colleges, they had different sets of friends outside Dalkey, Shane's from the Irish language groups in Trinity and Jennifer's arty crowd. The pair had discussed marriage and even building a house together in Wicklow, where Shane had a promise of some land.

Underneath the surface, however, Shane and Jennifer were vastly different. She knew that she had a lot of the world to see and a lot of people to meet, but he knew just one thing: Jennifer was his world.

In August 2007 the couple decided to take a break, and split for six weeks. But they got back together and their relationship continued, as intense as ever. Shane earned a good wage from his work in the Club, but he was renowned for being charitable. He regularly gave away money to beggars and had a particular empathy with the homeless. At his twenty-first birthday celebration, which was held in the Club, he placed a collection box for the Society of St Vincent de Paul on the bar and asked anyone who came to give to it rather than buy him a present. At Christmas he volunteered to help the homeless and even worked on Christmas Day to help feed a group that gathered at nearby Stradbrook Rugby Club. He didn't like people to talk about what he gave away and would get embarrassed if he was complimented for his generosity. Giving was easy for him because, with Jennifer by his side, Shane Clancy had everything he'd ever wanted.

Three years into the relationship, things weren't going so well. As young women do, Jennifer was changing as she went through college. The differences between her and Shane had deepened, and the divide caused by their separate college lives, circles of friends and interests had become harder to ignore. Jennifer was part of a very close class at the IADT. The members liked to socialise together regularly, hitting the city centre for nights out. Seb Creane – a popular and good-looking music lover – was one of her closest friends in the group. Often they would share a taxi home, as they lived in the same direction. They were just friends, but Shane became extremely jealous of the bright and handsome young man, whom he increasingly saw as a threat to his relationship with Jennifer.

Towards the end of 2008 Shane stopped working at the Club bar. The owners have never specified why they parted company with their barman, but it is understood that his attitude and brooding had become so intense that they felt they could no longer employ him. Things were going badly with Jennifer and his life was about to collapse. After New Year the couple's relationship practically petered out. When he suddenly suggested on 13 March 2009 that they end it, Jennifer was thrilled to get out without too much fuss. They agreed to meet and reassess things the following September. Jennifer hoped they could remain friends. She also hoped that he would pull himself together and go back to being the independent, hard-working individual she had met and fallen in love with three years before. Most of all, she wanted him to meet someone who felt as he did and move on.

But things were different for Shane. In fact, those who knew him would later surmise that he had hoped to call his girlfriend's bluff when he had suggested they split. In Shane Clancy's mind, he and Jennifer were meant to be together and nobody could possibly live up to her.

After the break-up, he regretted his rash decision and quickly realised that he wanted more than anything to win Jennifer back. He started to turn up where he knew she would be and beg her to go back to him. But Jennifer was adamant that what they had once had was gone. Besides, she was enjoying being single: she wanted to live a bit without having to report to anyone what she was doing. She had always had a large network of friends and now she could enjoy going out without having to consult Shane or tell him where she would be. To top it off, she was starting to notice Seb Creane on a different level and he seemed to like her too.

Shane was initially stunned by Jennifer's willingness to give up their relationship without a fight. He couldn't believe that she was doing so well without him. To make matters worse, she had decided to go to Thailand with friends. The trip was planned for June, around the same time that Shane had been planning to go to India to do charity work. He had signed up for it months earlier, and even after their split, Jennifer had organised a fundraiser for him at the Club – many of those who attended hadn't even known their relationship was over.

But behind the façade, Shane's behaviour had changed notably. At college he no longer showed the same interest in his subjects or his work for charity. He became more and more obsessed with Jennifer. She joked with her friends that he was getting to be a bit like a stalker and that she hoped he would move on, find another girl and forget about her, just as she was learning to live without him. By early May, Jennifer and Seb's relationship had deepened, but as they were part of a wide circle of close friends, they were initially reluctant to reveal that they were together.

Seb was in many ways the opposite of Shane. He was an easy-going guy and great fun. He was an avid photographer and musician, and he had a large number of friends. Like Jennifer, he had attended a fee-paying secondary school, St Gerard's in Bray, and he lived with his parents. Also like Jennifer, he didn't have the burden of paying rent, college fees or putting food on his table. He was a young guy enjoying the life of a student and he hadn't mapped out his future in the same way that Shane had. He had thrown himself into life and was happy to go wherever it would take him. He came from an extremely loving home and had an older brother, Dylan, whom he cited as one of his best friends. Seb was welcoming to everyone: nobody was excluded from his group or his company, and no one had a bad word to say about him. He was happy for Jennifer to do her own thing and wasn't overbearing. Life was good. Jennifer and Seb had got together before the end of the college year. They both had plans for the summer and were happy to leave things open: if they wanted to be together once they got back, so be it.

At the end of May, at a friend's birthday party, their group found out the pair were more than just friends. Jennifer immediately knew she had to tell Shane before he found out from someone else. The following day she told him about Seb Creane.

At that point, Shane Clancy changed utterly. Jennifer would later tell an inquest that everything about him, even his gait when he walked, was transformed, and he began to feel very sorry for himself.

Over the few days between hearing her news and when she left for Thailand, Shane bombarded her with texts and phone calls, trying desperately to prove to her how much he loved her. On 3 June, the day before her flight, she realised that things were very bad with him. At home, as she was packing, Shane arrived with presents for her birthday. Jennifer asked him to leave her alone and explained that she couldn't take the gifts. He refused to go away and sat in his car outside her home. When she again asked him to leave, he took off at speed, and she became worried that he would crash. She phoned him and discovered he was in the car, but just around the corner. The pair spoke for hours, and later that night a member of his family had to come to Dalkey to stay with him because he was so upset.

Jennifer hoped that while she was in Thailand, Shane would start to get over the relationship. But two weeks into the holiday she received emails from him, telling her he was on a world trip of his own. She phoned home and was told that he was in Thailand. Thankful that she had moved on to Laos and that her phone wasn't working, she was still bombarded with emails.

She also discovered that Shane had been hacking into her Facebook account. She changed her passwords, but his behaviour had ruined her holiday and she knew that things were serious.

While Jennifer had been away, Seb had been on holiday in Morocco with friends. Shane, on the other hand, had dropped out of his trip to India. Suas Educational Development had handpicked a small group of students deemed suitable for the trip and had earmarked Shane as one of their best choices. He had undergone months of training and orientation, and had fundraised for the group by packing bags in supermarkets in Dalkey and in Cornelscourt. The group were due to travel to Calcutta on 14 June. Shane had cited personal reasons for pulling out, giving no further explanation. His mother would say later that he had told his mentor he was feeling down about the break-up with Jennifer and that his trip had been deferred until the following year. She added that he was at home with her when he took a phone call telling him the trip had been put off. She had advised him to book a round-the-world ticket rather than spend the summer moping. Shane chose to visit a cousin in Thailand before heading on to Australia. His family hoped that the holiday would sort him out – they were not to know that he would bombard Jennifer with pleading emails.

Before he left, Shane visited his father and told him he didn't feel up to the Calcutta expedition. He said he had broken up with Jennifer but didn't want to talk about it. Later Patrick Clancy told the *Sunday Tribune*: 'He went to try and clear his head, to sort himself out. He was twenty-two and broken-hearted. When you're that age, you think it's the end of the world. He and Jen were a lovely couple; she's a lovely girl. They were very happy whenever I saw them together. He was besotted with her and she was besotted with him.'

Shane left for Thailand, but Patrick worried about him – so much so that he phoned his nephew out there to find out how his son was getting on. His nephew reported that Shane had been very quiet and seemed down when he first arrived but he had cheered up a little and was deep in a book on Barack Obama. The holiday was due to last weeks, but after a fortnight Shane returned. He hadn't used his ticket for

Australia. His depression had deepened but nobody knew that he had become dangerously fixated on Jennifer. He had started a series of letters to her, describing how they would 'walk hand in hand together in heaven'. He had written one on the plane to Thailand: if she ever read it, he noted, they would be together again.

On her return in July, Jennifer headed for Galway to keep out of Dalkey and away from Shane.

After his failed trip, Shane had confided in his mother that he couldn't get over his depression and couldn't get his break-up with Jennifer out of his head. She insisted he see the doctor and went with him to make sure he received whatever medication he required to get him through the bad patch. On their first visit, the doctor told him to go home, eat healthily and exercise. Three days later Leonie took him back to the surgery where he was prescribed an anti-depressant. He had been taking it for about a week when he swallowed the remaining three weeks' supply in one day, possibly an attempt at suicide. He told his mother what he had done, and two days later she took him to another GP. It was explained to the second doctor that Shane had taken a high dosage of the drug, but he was prescribed it again, in a lower dosage.

When Jennifer returned to Dalkey, she arranged to meet an old friend at the Ivory Bar. She hoped she wouldn't bump into Shane but the minute she walked into the bar, Shane was waiting for her. He came up to her and told her he would be out the back if she wanted to speak to him. The next day, Jennifer took him off her list of friends on her Facebook page.

On 15 August Shane made a last-ditch bid to get her back. It was a Saturday and she and her brother Luke were spending the day with their father, Jimmy, in his workplace at the Glen of the Downs, County Wicklow. As the evening drew in, Jimmy told Luke and Jennifer to hide, that Shane Clancy had arrived. Jennifer hid in the toilets for an hour-and-a-half while Jimmy tried to explain to Shane that he would have to move on with his life. During the conversation Shane told Jimmy that he had been put on the planet to be with Jennifer and that she was never going to find anyone who loved her as much as he did.

The next evening, Seb Creane had arranged to meet friends in the Eagle House pub in Glasthule. His parents were away in Cornwall on holidays and he had a 'free house'. Jennifer was going into town. The two had made a loose arrangement to hook up later in the evening and Jennifer would stay at Seb's house. That night she received a text from Seb, who told her that Shane was there.

In Glasthule, Seb and his best friends, twin brothers Gareth and Ross Cahill, had been surprised when they saw Shane Clancy sitting with a mutual friend of theirs in the bar when they arrived around ten o'clock. Shane was extremely quiet but the others chatted away and politely tried to include him. The group enjoyed a few pints, then decided to move on to the Queens pub in Dalkey, where there was a late-night club upstairs and they could party until the early hours. Although he wasn't drinking, Shane went ahead of the group with some girls who had joined them. The group had another few pints at the Queens, then made their way upstairs to the club. Most sat on couches near the door but Shane seemed to wander about on his own.

Some time after two a.m., the group decided to head for home. As they made their way out of the door Shane joined them. For the first time that night, he became animated and butted into the conversation as they talked about getting a taxi home, insisting that he would drive Seb, Gareth and Ross to Bray and save them the fare. While the lads were happy to jump into a cab, he was so insistent that they felt they had to accept his offer. They headed for a chipper while he walked the few minutes down the road to collect his car.

Ross sat in the front while Gareth and Seb were in the back. During the twenty-minute drive, Shane handled the car erratically and hit kerbs a number of times. Although he hadn't been drinking, the others were concerned by his reckless behaviour. He asked Seb where he lived and when Seb told him, he said, 'I know where you live.' Seb typed a message on his phone and showed it to Gareth:

```
He knows where I live, he'll have an
axe murderer after me.
```

The brothers told Shane to drop Seb off first, then leave them at their home, but again he became insistent: he told them he would drop them off first. The brothers got the impression that he wanted to be alone with Seb and perhaps have the conversation that everyone had avoided all night – the fact that Seb was now going out with Shane's ex-girlfriend.

At their house, Ross asked Seb to stay the night, but he said he'd rather sleep in his own bed. After they got out of the car the brothers texted Seb – they were worried:

```
Are you fucking crazy? You should have
definitely stayed here, that guy is not
right. At least get him to drop you off
at a house that ain't yours.
```

But Seb's kind nature would prove his undoing. Outside his parents' house in a quiet cul-de-sac, he thanked Shane for the lift and asked him if he wanted to come in for a cup of tea. It will never be known what the pair discussed in the house, but texts Shane sent to Jennifer indicated that his weird demeanour had intensified and that Seb had been frightened when Shane asked him for a knife or scissors to fix his shoes. He had told him to leave, which he did.

In the meantime, Jennifer hopped into a cab and headed for Cuala Grove to discuss the night's events with Seb, who knew he wouldn't be able to sleep after the time he had spent with Shane. In the sitting room, with *Pirates of the Caribbean* on the television, they discussed Shane and his increasingly bizarre stalking of Jennifer and now Seb.

While they talked, Shane Clancy was making his way to Dunnes. Some time after he had bought his block of knives, he texted Jennifer:

Jen, I did something stupid and I'm going to die now. Get Seb to help me.

Then he phoned her and started talking in gasps: 'I'm so cold. I'm going to die.' Over and over again he said, 'Get Seb to help me.' She asked him where he was, but he asked where she was. She told him she was just leaving town, but he said he knew she was lying. 'Are you in Bray, Shane?' she asked him. 'Are you outside?'

Seb spotted him outside the house and called to Jennifer. He walked outside and Shane approached him. He appeared to be injured. He was hobbling and walking slowly. Jennifer hung back while Seb tried to determine whether or not Shane really did need his help. Within seconds, all hell broke loose.

'What the fuck is that? Run, Jen! Run!' screamed Seb, as Shane lunged towards him with one of the knives. Jennifer raced into the sitting room and tried to barricade herself in, terrified by the screams she could hear in the hallway. As she cowered, the door broke open and Shane launched himself at her, kicking and punching, while she begged him to stop. Upstairs, Seb's brother Dylan and his girlfriend, Laura Mackey, woke up. Dylan jumped out of bed and saw his brother, seriously injured, crawling into their parents' bedroom. He could hear Jennifer grappling with someone. He rushed down the stairs to the hall, where he was immediately confronted by Shane, who was now brandishing one of the Creanes' kitchen knives. He began to attack Dylan, overpowering him and stabbing him again and again.

Within moments Dylan realised that the other man was trying to kill him and tried to hold him off. He looked around for something to arm himself with and saw his own keys lying on the hall table with his attached Swiss Army knife. He grabbed it and pulled it open with his teeth, breaking one in his panic, and held it to his attacker's face, threatening to stab him in the eye if he didn't let go. Shane retreated briefly, and Dylan hauled himself back up the stairs to where his brother was dying on the bedroom floor. Terrified, he ran back to his room where Laura was in deep shock and the couple barricaded themselves in.

In the meantim,e Shane had returned to the sitting room and again launched himself at Jennifer. He swung his fists at her. As he punched her, she noticed he was wearing a turquoise Puma hoodie. She remembered she had been with him when he bought it. She fell face forward on to the couch and he stabbed her in the back with such force that the handle of the knife broke off and the blade lodged between her shoulders. Somehow Jennifer pulled herself up and grabbed her mobile phone. Before she reached the back doo,r she had dialled her father's number. She never looked back as she clambered over the wall and landed in the next-door neighbour's garden.

John Stafford was in bed and woke to the sound of a girl screaming: 'I've been stabbed.' John jumped out of bed and looked out of the window. He saw Jennifer standing on top of a concrete outhouse. He ran out and helped her into his home. She was clutching her mobile phone and talking to her father.

While John ran next door, his partner Claire comforted Jennifer and spoke to her dad on the phone. She called an ambulance and the gardaí, while John went to help the Creane brothers.

When he got into the house, calling for Seb, he realised things were worse than he had thought. In the hall there were pools of blood that led up the stairway. Seb was slumped at the door of a bedroom. He was grey and appeared lifeless. John had some training in first aid, having done a course with the Order of Malta, and he tried to help his young neighbour before gardaí and the paramedics arrived and took over. As he made his way back to his own house he heard a paramedic say: 'This man is dead.'

Gardaí sealed off the scene as ambulance crews attended the injured, but Shane Clancy was nowhere to be seen. Dylan and Jennifer were rushed to hospital. Despite their horrendous injuries, both were able to give officers a brief outline of what had happened. Laura, too, did her best but she hadn't seen Clancy and had never left the bedroom while the events unfolded below her. She was taken to hospital suffering from severe shock. Clancy's car was still outside the house but he had disappeared.

Two teams of gardaí were sent out, one to knock on Patrick Clancy's door and a second to Leonie Fennell's house in Wicklow. The man in charge of the investigation, Detective Inspector Frank Keenaghan, knew two things: first, his men had to manage the scene of the crime and seal it off so that absolutely no forensic evidence was destroyed until the expert teams arrived, and second, they had to find Shane Clancy.

Patrick Clancy was asleep in bed when he heard the purposeful knock on his door that would change his life for ever. He opened it to find two uniformed officers, who politely introduced themselves and told him that his son's car had been discovered earlier that morning outside a house in Bray where a young man had been fatally stabbed and two others had been injured. Patrick would later describe how he knew immediately that if Shane had been responsible for the stabbings, there was no way he was still alive. 'I knew he could not live with himself,' he said. Officers asked Patrick to call phone his son's mobile but it went straight to voicemail.

In Wicklow the same scenario was playing out at Leonie Fennell's home, where she was telling officers that they had got it wrong and that Shane's car must have been stolen.

As morning broke, the grim task of informing Seb's parents, Nuala and Jimmy, was left to Keenaghan. He had to call and tell them that one of their sons was dead and a second was fighting for his life in hospital. He would later describe it as one of the most difficult things he had ever had to do in his career. The Creanes made immediate arrangements to come home.

Back at Cuala Grove, forensic experts had begun to arrive and as they examined the scene, they slowly picked their way out to the back of the house and into the garden where Jennifer had made her escape. There, at the end of the garden, hidden in some shrubbery, they discovered another body. Slumped in a crouched position, Shane Clancy was dead. A carving knife lay on the ground beneath him. Officers were alerted and a murder hunt became a murder-suicide enquiry.

From the outset officers on the case, many of whom were highly experienced in the business of death, were stunned. Clancy had no history of crime, and while it was clear that he had become obsessed with his ex-girlfriend, few could believe the extent of the violence he had perpetrated. Not only had he killed Seb, but his attacks on Jennifer and Dylan were so severe that it was obvious he had attempted to murder them too. Most shocking of all was that he had killed himself in such a bizarre and violent fashion. While investigators would have to wait for the official postmortem results from the State Pathologist, the injuries to his body indicated that he had tried to stab himself a number of times before he had wedged the knife into the ground and then brought his body down on it. It would have taken time and effort and was one of the most unusual methods of suicide many officers had ever seen.

Teams were deployed to Wicklow and Dun Laoghaire, where Shane's stunned parents were told that his body had been discovered. At eleven thirty a.m. Deputy State Pathologist Declan Gilsenen arrived at the scene. He wouldn't finish his work until early afternoon, when a hearse arrived to take the two bodies away from the scene. By then the media were swarming around Bray and the name Shane Clancy was about to become etched in Irish criminal history. By Sunday afternoon, most who were working on the story realised that his actions at Cuala Grove had been sparked by romantic rivalry with Seb Creane. They were also working to piece together the events that had led up to his attack: he had appeared to have put himself in Seb's company the previous night, dropped him home and then returned to Cuala Grove after arming himself. As the pair had been out in a pub and the murder had happened in the early hours of the morning, it would have been easy to jump to the conclusion that the attack had been drink-fuelled but, like so many aspects of the case, that didn't add up: reporters were told that Shane Clancy did not drink. Drugs were fast being ruled out too, as he had no history of taking illegal narcotics.

Detectives, who would have to deliver a file on the case to a coroner, were attempting to find out exactly how Clancy had got into Seb's home, but they had no way of questioning their two main witnesses, Dylan and Jennifer, as they were too badly injured to talk. Teams of officers were sent out to those who had been with Seb the night before, and as they waited to question those in the house, they started to take statements from the friends who had been with him in what had turned out to be the last few hours of his life.

A search was also carried out at Shane Clancy's bedsit. There, officers found eight letters addressed to Jennifer Hannigan placed neatly on the mantelpiece. They were the letters that he had been writing since he had split with her and included the one he had penned on the plane to Thailand. The content was disturbing and showed the depths of his obsession with his ex-girlfriend. One had been written as far back as May. Beside them, there was a note for his mother in which he apologised for what he had to do.

By Sunday evening Jim and Nuala Creane were back in Ireland and being looked after by friends. Gardaí advised them not to go to their house, as it would be far too traumatic for them.

At St Vincent's Hospital Dylan was stabilising, and while he was seriously ill – one stab had punctured a lung – it looked as though he would make a full recovery. Jennifer was due to be operated on but medics believed there was no reason that she, too, wouldn't return to full health.

The post-mortem report, released to officers on Monday, found that Seb had died when the knife had severed the main artery to his heart. It was exactly the same injury that had killed Clancy – but only after he had made nineteen attempts to stab himself to death in the garden. Officers continued to try to establish a firm motive for the savage attack, and as a result of information from Leonie Fennell, they decided to do toxicology tests to see if what she was saying about the anti-depressants Clancy had been prescribed might throw light on what he had done. Leonie was insistent that his actions must have been caused by the drugs he had been prescribed – he had already taken an overdose – because they were so out of character. She told officers that he had only started taking the medication two weeks before the murder. 'Shane wouldn't have hurt a fly,' she said. 'He was never violent. There was nothing wrong with him before he started taking the medication. He was perfectly normal. It was the medication that made him do what he did.'

The officers knew that toxicology results could take weeks, if not months, to come back, but they also knew they had to examine every aspect of the case and could not ignore such vital information. At the same time, they weren't so sure that Shane Clancy had been 'perfectly normal' until he was prescribed the drug. The letters and evidence they were collecting from friends and acquaintances showed that his behaviour had been unusual for a long period before he had been prescribed the medication and very much focused on the girl who had been lucky to escape with her life.

As the days wore on, tributes were paid to Seb Creane as friends and lecturers from college poured out their sympathies to his family. He was described as a perfect gentleman and a cheerful soul, who had loved life and was facing a promising career as a photographer or an artist. Composer Phil Coulter said that Seb was almost part of his family, having been one of the closest and oldest friends of his own eldest son Daragh: 'He's the kind of lad that any father would be proud to have as a son, the kind of lad any father would be happy to have his daughter bring home and introduce as a boyfriend. He's a real sweet kid.' He dismissed reports that the tragedy had happened after a drunken night: nothing could be further from the truth. 'Seb was not a party animal. He was anything but an all-night boozer. That's exactly the wrong, wrong image of Seb Creane.' Coulter went on Joe Duffy's *Liveline* show to describe Seb and the violence of his death. 'My heart bleeds for Seb and Dylan's parents, really and truly, and for the parents of the other lad, who I didn't know at all. Their grief is equal, if not worse, because of the detail of the story. It's the sort of thing that, twenty years ago, would have brought this country to a standstill. We have become as a nation and a race brutalised: we have become immune to this type of violence and it's a scary thing.'

Shortly after Coulter's interview, a friend of Clancy's, who would only give his name as Philip, rang in to say that he was a 'great, great young man . . . It's a shock to everybody, to all my peers. It's, like, where do you see yourself tomorrow? One day everything is fine, then the next it is just blown up into pieces. You take your life in your hands every day. You have to live your life one day at a time and do your best for the day that is in it.'

While that caller did not want to identify himself to the nation as a friend or defender of Clancy, those who gathered in the Church of the Assumption in Dalkey on the Thursday morning for his funeral mass had to. Outside, a huge media gathering captured images of his family and friends, who had turned out in their droves to mourn his passing. Inside the church, a young Facebook generation held one another and looked for answers to what had turned their kind, caring friend into a killer. Patrick Clancy joined his ex-wife Leonie, with her husband Tony and their children, in the front pew.

Father John McDonagh, the parish priest, talked about a stunned community trying to come to terms with events that had been totally out of character for Shane Clancy. 'A young man held in such high regard among you that last Sunday's awful news was, and is, incredible to you, so very hard, if not impossible, to understand and to come to terms with.' He described Shane as a devoted man of charity: 'Everyone I spoke to who knew him referred to his commitment to charity ventures and causes.' Prayers were said for the Clancy family as well as the families of Seb and Jennifer, and the congregation were asked to pray for those suffering from depression. 'Understandably we are heartbreakingly shocked by the psychotic state and destructive frenzy into which his mind suddenly entered, so uncharacteristically, it would seem. Amid all the talk and comment, the truth is there may be a few gifted people in Ireland who, in their professional capacity, understand such awful transitions in a young man's life, who can interpret and understand what baffles and mystifies the rest of us,' he said. 'The Shane that many of you knew and loved was overtaken by a cruel darkness early on Sunday last, bringing great tragedy to other lovely families as well as his own.'

But as the congregation made its way to Shanganagh Cemetery where Shane was to be buried, another priest was set to insist that his actions could not be excused or whitewashed, or hidden behind the veil of mental illness.

Father Fergus O'Donoghue, a family friend of the Creanes and the editor of the Jesuit Order's review publication, *Studies*, issued a statement saying that as long as a person had free will, they were responsible for their actions. 'What is disturbing is the element of premeditation, of going home and discovering where Sebastian lived and then going to buy the knives. We don't like to use the word "sin" nowadays and we like to find a psychological explanation. This doesn't do,' he said. 'Anybody in any situation has free will and we have a choice as to how we can act.' He called on the government to review the easy access people had to knives at any time of the night and criticised how 'a culture of consumerism' meant that people were able to buy what they wanted whenever they wanted it without question. 'Knives are so freely available and we don't seem to have understood the growing extent of knife crime. These things tend to come from Britain and it's an established thing in Britain that several dozen young men die from knife crime every year, and now it is over here.'

He wasn't the first to talk about the spread of knife crime. Others blamed the knife-crime culture for the tragedy in Bray. Fine Gael's spokesman on justice, Charlie Flanagan, talked about a dramatic surge in knife killings and a possible epidemic of them in Ireland. While gardaí were not convinced there was anything like an epidemic in Ireland – and figures showed it had dropped significantly – nobody could argue that Shane Clancy's purchase of knives in Dunnes Stores was anything but a key aspect of the case.

While they were still waiting for the toxicology results to discover how much of the anti-depressant he had had in his system, many admitted that Clancy had shown a worrying amount of premeditation to kill. Investigating officers now knew that he had gone out of his way to find Seb hours before he drove a knife into his heart, and statements from the Cahill brothers indicated that he was adamant he would find out where Seb lived when he drove him home.

While gardaí were adamant that they would investigate every avenue, it was increasingly apparent that the only person who could really explain what had driven him to do what he had done was dead, and that the Creanes and Jennifer Hannigan were facing a lifetime of unanswered questions.

In the meantime Jim and Nuala Creane were facing a day

no parent should have to experience, as they set about organising Seb's funeral. Just four days after Shane Clancy was buried, his victim was laid out in a wicker coffin in the chapel at his old school, St Gerard's, before he was removed to the church in Bray.

On the same day, an interview with Patrick Clancy featured in the *Irish Examiner*. He said he was upset with Father O'Donoghue's comments: 'I still don't believe my son was in his right mind. Shane could never have lived with what he had done. Shane was a pacifist and I don't think he knew what rage and anger were and when it hit him, it was too late. A few seconds and everything was gone . . . Shane loved Jennifer. She was everything to him. Jennifer is a beautiful girl and a beautiful person. I don't think Shane came to terms with it when he left her . . . A broken heart is a very strange thing. I think that Shane felt angry and sad but he couldn't express his feelings and instead suppressed them.'

The following morning, Jennifer joined hundreds of mourners at Seb's funeral as his mother made a poignant and moving tribute to her beloved son. 'I notice that both boys who died were twenty-two, both had the same initials, both were about to enter their final year in college and looked set, even in these recessionary times, to have fruitful careers . . . So many similarities. Yet on the morning of 16 August, my God of small things said to me, one boy represented the light, the other the darkness.' She urged mourners to channel thoughts of happiness and comfort to Jennifer who, she told them, felt responsible for what had happened. 'She blames herself. Make her heart feel that happiness.'

During her address, she described her beloved son as a charmer with curly hair and brown eyes. Then she spoke about what had happened in her home: 'Dylan, Seb, Jen and Laura faced a presence of demonic proportions that manifested itself through Shane Clancy.' For fifteen minutes she spoke of her devastation at her son's death.

When she had finished a lone mourner stood up and clapped loudly. Within seconds the whole congregation were on their feet, moved by a mother trying to make sense of her loss. It was only eight days since her child had been killed.

As the weeks passed and the garda investigation continued, Leonie Fennell was becoming more and more insistent that her son's name had been blackened and that he had been driven insane by the tablets he had taken. A month after the attacks, she penned a letter to *The Gerry Ryan Show*, which was read out on air: 'I loved my son and will always be proud of him. What happened to Shane to turn him into such an unrecognisable person that night? Was it because he didn't drink or do drugs that his system couldn't cope with the anti-depressants? Or can depression melt your brain if it gets that bad? Will we ever know? All I know is that Shane wouldn't hurt a fly but turned unrecognisable that night for some reason.' She said she wanted listeners to know who her son was before the events of 16 August. 'Shane had it all. A stable home, a lovely flat in Dalkey, his own car, college going well and family and friends who loved him unconditionally. He gave half his grant money to a homeless man he befriended, which meant we had to pay his rent, but that was normal.' She said her son had begun to show signs of depression in the months before the attack but when he returned early from his round-the-world trip she had brought him to the doctor. 'I made him get anti-depressants, which he didn't want to take but I insisted. It's very hard to watch your six-foot son with tears dripping down his face.'

As the garda investigation wound down and the Wicklow

Coronor had been furnished with all statements, reports and toxicology results, it was decided that separate inquests would be held for Shane Clancy and Seb Creane. Shane's was heard first, by East Wicklow Coroner Dr Cathal Louth, in April 2010. Statements made by Jennifer, Dylan Creane, Ross and Gareth Cahill were read, outlining the events of the night. In his written testimony Gareth described how Clancy was very quiet all night and drove aggressively on the way home. He described the text message he had sent to Seb, warning him to get out at a house that wasn't his own after the brothers had been dropped off.

Jennifer Hannigan was visibly shaken in the witness box as she told the court what had happened. She said that she had gone out with Clancy from January 2006, but by March 2009 the relationship had run its course. 'Shane was the first to say it,' she said. When she had begun dating Seb, she said Clancy had been instantly jealous, and from that day on, he had changed in the way he 'walked, talked, everything'. The day before the attack her father had spoken to Clancy when he had arrived at his work. 'Shane said I was put on this planet to be with him and no one was ever going to love me as much as him,' she said. On the night of the attack, she had had a text from her boyfriend Seb, saying that Clancy had shown up in his company and that the night had been 'surreal'. After she arrived at Seb's house she had had a text from Shane saying he 'did something stupid and was going to die'. She rang him but realised he was outside Seb's house. 'While I was on the phone, Seb opened the door and Shane was outside. Seb thought he was really hurt. He was walking like an old man, pretending to be injured.' After stabbing Seb, Shane had turned his attention to her. She told the court: 'I was shouting at Shane, "Don't do this, Shane, it's me." As I got on to the couch, Shane stabbed me in the back. I said to myself, "I am not going to die." I got my phone and rang my dad as I was running away.'

Dylan recounted how he awoke that night to hear voices downstairs. He initially went back to sleep but then was woken by screaming and could hear his brother saying, 'I've been stabbed.' He said he ran downstairs to find Seb with blood on his shirt and then recalled a person coming towards him, saying, 'It's okay, it's okay.' In shocking detail he described how the person grabbed him and overpowered him. He felt no pain, just thumps on his back and left side. Then he saw the knife in the man's hand: 'I realised this guy was trying to kill me.' He described how he grabbed his keys and persuaded Clancy to back off. At that point he had been stabbed nine times.

While their statements were shocking in the extreme, it was the evidence relating to the anti-depressants in Clancy's system that would prove insightful into the state of his mind, but also more controversial. The inquest heard that he had had 'toxic to fatal' levels of the drug in his system: 3.1 mg of Cipramil was discovered in his blood, which is fifteen times the upper therapeutic dose. Dr Declan Gilsenan, who had performed the postmortems, told the coroner that the UK Committee on Safety in Medicine had advised that the type of drug found in Clancy's system, an SSRI, shouldn't be used by anyone under eighteen as 'trials suggest harmful outcomes'. He said that one theory on the drug suggested there may be a danger period at the start of treatment because before it lifts depression, it alters a person's ability to make decisions.

Professor David Healy of Cardiff University said Cipramil was known to cause 'suicidal and homicidal thoughts' among a minority of people. He believed that Clancy had had an adverse reaction to it and should never have been prescribed it. Healy is a long-time campaigner for anti-depressant safety and the author of *Let Them Eat Prozac*. He is regularly called on to give evidence in cases where anti-depressants are used. Leonie Fennell told the court that her son had slipped into depression after the break-up of his relationship and was 'miserable with the weight of a broken heart'. She admitted that she had persuaded him to go to the doctor on 18 July – just two months before the attacks – but he was told to go away, exercise and eat properly. He showed no improvement, so she brought him back on 22 July and the doctor prescribed a month's supply of Cipramil. On 5 August he had taken the overdose. Two days later, she had taken him to a locum doctor and was surprised when Shane received another prescription for the same drug.

The jury at Wicklow Courthouse rejected an option of death by suicide and returned an open verdict that Clancy had died of self-inflicted injuries.

After the inquest, Professor of Clinical Psychiatry Patricia Casey read a statement expressing the College of Psychiatry of Ireland's disappointment at the coroner's decision not to allow it to give evidence. Later Lundbeck, the drug manufacturers, disputed the evidence given and the claims made about the drug, saying it had been used by 130 million patients worldwide: 'Extensive scientific studies have shown that there is no evidence linking citalopram to violent behaviour. Trials show it has the potential to reduce, rather than provoke, irritability, aggression and violent behaviour.'

A month later, at Seb Creane's inquest, his parents issued a statement strongly criticising the inquest process. They said they should have been allowed to ask questions at Clancy's inquest. 'Everything that took place on 16 August was known before the day was out. Nonetheless, we have had to worry about and endure the gruesome and futile ritual of two coroners' inquests, which have done nothing to advance knowledge of the facts,' they said, in a statement read by their solicitor. They also wanted to challenge the 'assumption' that Clancy's actions were as the result of prescribed medication. 'Let us not forget what happened here. Seb was stalked by a person who, having manoeuvred his way into our home, left, armed himself and returned some time later to complete his objective. By playing on Seb's better nature, he once again gained access to the house, killed Seb, attempted to kill Jen and then Dylan, before withdrawing to kill himself. We cannot comprehend that an attempt was made to ascribe fault to prescribed medication without any corresponding attempt being made to consider all other factors. Healing for all parties will inevitably be difficult, but no true healing can ever be founded on denial.'

While the Creanes have rarely made any public statements about the tragedy that unfolded in their happy home that night, they have held to their view that the Clancys are in denial about their son's actions. For her part Leonie Fennell has continued in her campaign against anti-depressants and has launched a blog for better awareness of the side effects of the drugs. She is raising funds, in Shane's name, to help homeless people and has collected more than €2,200 through friends and family of the student who was known in college as 'Croi Mor' (big heart). The money will be given to the Simon Community. On her blog, she has posted numerous pictures of Shane smiling and enjoying life with his family and out with friends.

> Shane was the nicest, kindest, funniest guy you could meet. He was loved by all his friends and family, and adored by his younger siblings. He took them out every weekend. He babysat for us all the time and even minded them when we went to New York for a weekend.

We put him down as guardian and never had to worry about what would happen to them because Shane was so reliable . . . He had lots of really good friends and always had a job. This is the Shane that we all knew and loved. He was working one night in the Conradh [the Irish pub on Harcourt Street] and this guy came in and tried to hit a girl. He was so upset that someone could hit a girl. We said, 'Why didn't you box him?' and Shane said that he didn't do violence and he wasn't going down to that guy's level. He wasn't capable of hurting anyone or himself. So when the gardaí said there was no mistake and it was Shane involved in the events of 16 August, I knew something was wrong somewhere.

What was 'wrong somewhere' will continue to form a larger debate on the safety of psychiatric drugs and the monitoring of them in patients.

For the Creanes, a grave in Mayo is all they have left of their beautiful son. Dylan will never see his brother again and the horrors that must have played out in young Jennifer's mind will live with her forever. Shane Clancy may have believed that he was put on this planet to love Jennifer Hannigan, but when he unleashed his rage on a hot summer's night, he ensured that she would never forget him.

8

'HELP . . . HE'S KILLING US'
Arthur McElhill and The Omagh Tragedy

The McElhill family had largely kept to themselves since they had arrived to live at 4 Lammy Crescent. Neighbours knew little of their background, other than that he was a local from Omagh and she was originally from Cavan. They rarely socialised but appeared, like any other family on the estate, to work hard to pay the bills and rear their children as best they could. They had their rows, and it was widely suspected that Arthur sometimes hit Lorraine. She was often seen with a black eye or other injuries that, if questioned, she laughed off. She was considered a chatty woman and it was said that she often spoke of Arthur and how fantastic he was.

Lorraine had been pregnant when she had moved into the house, without Arthur, in late 1999, with her then five-year-old daughter Caroline. Five months later Sean was born, and some time after that, Arthur arrived to live with his family. Nobody paid much attention to their situation. Many presumed they had had their differences for a while and evidently got over them. Lorraine told some neighbours she loved babies and wanted a big family. Three years after Sean had come along, she had a second daughter, Bellina, followed by another three-year gap before Clodagh and then, ten months later, James appeared. She certainly had her hands full.

Like most of the other kids on Lammy Crescent, the McElhill children played on the road and attended St Conor's Primary School, which was located directly beside their rented home. By now Caroline had moved up to the Sacred Heart College where she was an avid camogie player. She had plenty of friends, who often visited the house, and seemed to be a normal teenager, concerned about her looks and boys.

Lorraine busied herself looking after her brood and was rarely seen out without a string of children in buggies, on bikes or just skipping along behind her. She had her work cut out, especially with the two little ones being so close in age. On the estate they were known as the 'Irish Twins' and a few of the other women had remarked that Lorraine wasn't the first and wouldn't be the last to find herself in that situation.

From the outside, Arthur appeared to be a hands-on father. He worked for local landowner James Crammond, who employed him on his farm, but he would often be seen in the evenings rounding up his children for bed – which was strictly at seven p.m. He was a big man and must have weighed at least eighteen stone. He was known to drink but never in the local pubs with the rest of the men. Neighbours would report, in the aftermath of the tragedy, that it was not unusual to hear Arthur's raised voice. But the altercation that neighbour Lee Anne Duffy overheard on the night in question was different. It was a blazing row and, despite the late hour, it didn't sound as if it was going to abate.

When Lee Anne was woken at four forty-five a.m. by raised voices, red lights and the sound of car doors slamming, she had quietly slipped out of bed, so as not to wake the rest of her family, gone to the window and pulled the curtain back just enough to see out. Outside the McElhills', she could just make out the figure of a big, bulky man standing at the rear passenger side of the family's people carrier. Although she couldn't see his face, she was sure from his size that it was Arthur. As she turned to go back to bed she heard a loud voice shout, 'You can't run, you fat bitch!'

Within minutes other neighbours had woken abruptly to what was to become a night of unthinkable horror on Lammy Crescent. No one who witnessed it will ever forget it. Screams of raw terror cut through the freezing air. All along the street, front doors swung open and neighbours staggered from their homes. To their horror, they saw a fireball and clouds of black smoke engulf number 4.

Frantically, wearing little but their night attire, people jumped into action and tried to save the family from the inferno. Next door, Gary Taggart rushed outside when he heard the screams and looked up at the blazing house. Arthur was standing at an upstairs window. Stephen Mullan could hear Lorraine screaming for help and saw Arthur, too, his face in his hand, thumping the glass with his fist.

Brothers Mark and John McGlinn acted quickly: their family ran a window-cleaning business. They grabbed one of their ladders and ran to the rescue, acutely aware that five children were trapped. The pair threw the ladder against the outside of the house and Mark made his way up the rungs towards the first floor. He could see Arthur at the window and roared at him to smash it. With the flames beating past his head, he screamed. 'Grab the ladder! Get out! Get the children out!' Arthur was hunkered down to sill level in the bedroom, but he didn't speak when Mark shouted and banged on the window in a desperate attempt to pull him out of his state of shock. As Mark squinted against the blistering heat coming from above his head, he saw his neighbour blinking and looking around out of the window for a few seconds. Then he looked back into the room, into the flames.

In the background Lorraine was still screaming, but there was no sound from the children. 'Arthur! Arthur! Grab the ladder!' he tried one last time. But suddenly, with black smoke billowing around his eighteen-stone frame, Arthur turned around and walked purposely back into the fire.

As panic ensued and the fire gained momentum, roaring around the upstairs rooms and the roof, the emergency services skidded into Lammy Crescent and firefighters started to tackle the blaze. They had been contacted not only by the neighbours but had also received a 999 call from inside the house.

Fire crew Commander David Canning was one of the first at the scene. He would later tell an inquest that nothing in his lengthy career could have prepared him for the graphic scenes that greeted him that night. As his crew tried to bring the blaze under control with high-powered hoses, firefighters Adrian Clarke and Thomas Logue were first to gain entry to the property. Wearing protective breathing apparatus and special suits, they battled their way through the front door and into the hall. Aware that the family were likely to be on the second floor, they tried to make their way up the stairs but had to give up. The officers rushed for a ladder. Logue, despite burns to his arm, and Clarke struggled on against the flames.

When they eventually got to the upper floor, the fire was so intense that the building was in danger of collapsing on itself. 'Get out! The roof's coming in!' shouted Clarke to his colleague, as Logue stared in disbelief at the orange glow on the ceiling. But Clarke was right and, hearing the roof rumble, Logue scrambled back down the ladder and the pair retreated outside. The flames were so hot, they appeared white and, from experience, Logue knew that nobody could still be alive in the house.

Time and time again the firefighters thought they had got the blaze under control but it would reignite and, again, they would train their hoses on it.

When the units had at last put out the blaze, officers rushed back inside to search the house. But they knew in their hearts that nobody could have survived, that the smoke alone would have rendered anyone unconscious within minutes. Logue made his way into the large main bedroom and felt across a double bed with his hand. 'Odd,' he muttered. The bed appeared smooth as if it hadn't been slept in.

Later he explained: 'I was searching by touch. I felt the bed covers had not been disturbed. It was obvious it hadn't been slept in.' Through the wreckage and in the strange blackness from the thick smoke, firefighters moved cautiously through the bedrooms, careful with their footing so the floors didn't collapse.

In the smallest bedroom, just above the living room, they found two adult bodies, one on top of the other, lying on the floor. A child lay in its cot where it had been safely tucked earlier that evening. Three more children were discovered together in a second bedroom. A smouldering skull was all that was left on the bottom bunk. In the blackened remains of the largest child's little hand was what looked like a mobile phone, in the other what appeared to be a set of rosary beads. In the third bedroom, where baby James had slept, a firefighter saw what he thought was a doll. Black and melted. It was later identified as the ten-month-old infant, James.

Downstairs other horrors awaited David Canning and his team. Smoke-stained photos of the children were hanging on the walls of the rooms and his officers could still make out the smiling faces that had once laughed and played in this charred grave. In a bag, five bottles of formula milk had somehow survived the fire.

By morning the news of the fire was all over Omagh and local radio was reporting the tragedy that had thrown the town back into the news for all the wrong reasons. Nine years earlier, the eyes of the world had turned to Omagh when a Real IRA bomb killed twenty-nine people, including a woman pregnant with twin girls. Omagh was still raw from those barbaric murders, and now that same stillness, that same silence hung over it, like a shroud, once again.

Neighbours comforted one another with cups of tea as they tried to make sense of what had happened and how, in an instant, a family could have been wiped out in such tragic circumstances. Initial reports spoke of a quiet family who were well liked. Arthur was said to have been so distraught at the fate of his family that he had refused help for himself and gone back to be with them in their dying moments. Speculation about what caused the dreadful accident was rife – an electrical fault or a chip pan was blamed.

By eight a.m. an initial briefing from the firefighters to the police was that the blaze had not been started maliciously. They believed it to have been the result of a slow burn that had started upstairs. But as the investigators continued to comb the wreckage, they became concerned that the initial assessment was wrong and that perhaps the unthinkable had happened. Scorched skirting boards inside the front hall behind the door, usually the sign of an accelerant, raised eyebrows. Then they discovered that the windows and doors were all bolted from the inside.

Many at the scene, with years of experience in firefighting, couldn't make sense of how such an intense blaze could have started so quickly. As they picked their way through the ruins, it became obvious that the fire had intensified up the stairs and on to the second floor at an incredible rate. But how could it have become so powerful so suddenly? And why did the seat of the fire appear to be in a bedroom? As fire analysts were called in to examine the scene, it soon became clear why this was no ordinary house fire, and why nobody who had perished that night had had a chance of survival.

As soon as the traces of petrol were discovered in the burning embers of the terraced house, even hardened officers were left numb. Their investigations would later uncover that, at the height of the blaze, temperatures inside the house had reached at least 700 degrees centigrade – hot enough to melt glass light bulbs. The status of the investigation by the Police Service of Northern Ireland (PSNI), under Detective Superintendent Norman Baxter, immediately changed to murder, and Baxter was left with the grim task of briefing his officers. They were now looking for a person who had purposely torched a house containing seven people.

Outside, neighbours in Lammy Crescent were beginning to realise that something was very wrong, and rumours started to circulate that the fire might have been set deliberately. In the cold light of day it appeared more than odd that Arthur had refused help from Mark McGlinn and hadn't tried to fetch his children when the ladder was resting on the sill. Rumours that many had heard before, but brushed off as cruel gossip, resurfaced – and this time with far more significance. Friends of friends were quoted as having seen a woman who had caused a scene at McElhill's home a few weeks ago by accusing him of sex abuse. The same friends of friends had seen the police there on a number of occasions.

Newsrooms searched for pictures of the victims and a photograph taken just a few months ago at baby James's christening was unearthed. It showed the family smiling and happy: Lorraine, Caroline, Sean, Bellina, Clodagh, baby James, in his mother's arms, and the chortling Arthur, looking for all the world like the archetypal jolly fat dad. It was a picture of family harmony and benign innocence, and for parents across the country it spoke louder than words, louder than the pictures of the burned-out house.

As the day wore on, journalists and news crews descended on Lammy Crescent and quickly realised there was more to this 'accidental' house fire than met the eye. On the estate, those who had tried to help the family during the blaze recalled hearing a row minutes before the inferno had taken hold. They spoke of the unusual image of Arthur at the window, turning back into the flames. Some told reporters of the incident at the house when a woman had accused him of having sex with her teenage daughter and called him a pervert.

Inside the house, investigators were now convinced the blaze had been started deliberately. Fire analysts were flown in from the UK to help find out what had happened. Like pieces of a jigsaw, nuggets of information began to come together and a sinister picture began to emerge of the jolly giant in the photograph. Was it true that Arthur had been a sex offender? Was he a paedophile? How had he lived in their midst with such a secret? Why was a teenage girl staying at the house? Had Lorraine found out and was she about to leave him?

Outside the house, parents wept and children, confused and frightened, left teddies and flowers for their friends. A steady stream of mourners arrived to pay tribute to the family. Some offered a prayer. Others simply wept, lost for words at the enormity of what had happened. The sickly whiff of wet embers hung in the air outside the skeletal, blackened remains of the house. Beside it, the school car park, from which Caroline, Sean and Bellina had happily skipped into their classrooms, had become an unfamiliar site of police vehicles and a crane, which investigators were using to access the upstairs bedrooms. Amid the pile of flowers and letters wrapped in cellophane, one little boy had placed a note for Sean: 'You were my bestest friend in the classroom. You were the best Supermouse too. Sean: Hope you're playing football with the angels in heaven.'

As they gathered in groups, many whispered about Arthur's dark past. Some said he had been convicted of a sex attack on a girl when he was in his twenties and later raped another young girl after breaking into her home. But surely those who lived beside him would have known if he had had any such a criminal record?

Behind the scenes, officers under Chief Superintendent Baxter were being mobilised and briefed about the task that lay ahead. They had to piece together the last movements of the family, establish if anyone else might have been involved in setting the fire, then try to ascertain if Arthur was responsible and what had driven him to wipe out his family. Baxter also had to attempt to quell the rumours that were by now rife in Omagh. He needed his team to stay focused and separate fact from fiction.

On the Thursday afternoon, less than thirty-six hours after the blaze, he made the decision to face the media and confirm to the public that he was heading a murder enquiry. The chief of the PSNI's Serious Crime Squad stood grim-faced outside the house on Lammy Crescent as he announced the launch of the inquiry, which was to be led by Detective Superintendent

Tim Hanley and manned by thirty detectives. 'We have now moved to the position where we are saying, "This is a crime scene, and we have commenced a murder investigation,"' he announced. 'This is one of the most tragic and devastating murder investigations the PSNI has had to encounter, with the loss of so many young lives. Our initial forensic examination of the home established there was a significant quantity of accelerant in the property.'

At Lammy Crescent, he was flanked by the Deputy First Minister of the Northern Ireland Assembly, Martin McGuinness, who attempted to offer his sympathies to the community: 'There must be a certain amount of fear within the community. But the community will come through this and hopefully the investigation will reveal the full information about what happened here so the fears of the people can be allayed. The best way to expedite this inquiry is for people to co-operate with the police.'

At that point the PSNI were only looking at two possibilities. The first was that the fire had been started by someone inside the house, and the second, that it had been started by someone who had got into the house. But there were no obvious signs of a break-in and the finger of suspicion pointed firmly at Arthur.

Sixty hours after they had arrived to conduct their painful sifting through the debris of a family's life, forensic examiners completed their job. Outside, friends, teachers and children gathered as two white vans removed the remains of Arthur, Lorraine and the children. Emotions were still so raw that many doubled over, racked with sobs, and had to be led away by their families. Caroline's classmates from the Sacred Heart College formed a guard of honour. They had been receiving counselling since the news first broke that their friend and her family had perished.

As the days moved on, a clearer picture of Arthur McElhill's background began to emerge. What came out terrified those who had lived beside him, unaware of who he really was. It seemed, if the papers could be believed, that McElhill was indeed a sex offender with a leaning towards young teenage girls, and had had a criminal record before he had ever come to live at Lammy Crescent. Reports suggested that he was twice convicted of sexual assaults on females, receiving a two-year suspended sentence – having pleaded fragile mental health – for indecent assault on a woman after entering her home in County Tyrone in 1993, and a second sentence of three years of which he served eighteen months, for the indecent assault of a seventeen-year-old girl in 1998. Both women had been sleeping and had woken to find McElhill's huge frame looming over them. Newspaper sources said that he was indeed on the sex offenders' register and had a history of suicide attempts; he had even spent time in a psychiatric hospital. They said he was a depressed alcoholic who frequently beat Lorraine. In one paper, one of his two victims said she had been living in fear since he had attacked her in 1993: 'When I heard the news about the fire I felt sickened. I was scared of him all my life. I'm so sad for the lady and the children. I had always felt concerned for them because I knew what he was like and what he was capable of.' She also described how McElhill had tried to suffocate her during the attack.

Those who knew him to talk to on the estate struggled to believe that he was capable of such violence, but as the days passed, the newspapers churned out more and more stories about his past and about what had happened on the night of the fire. They painted a picture of an evil sadist disguised as an ordinary family man. Had he rounded his children up and doused their nightclothes in petrol before setting fire to them? Had he tied them up and strapped them to their beds so they had no way of escaping? Had he stockpiled petrol? Was Lorraine pregnant with their sixth child? Was she trying to leave him on the night of the fire?

A fortnight after the blaze, a bitter dispute over where the bodies should be buried had broken out between the McElhill and McGovern families. At Belfast Mortuary in Forster Green Hospital, officials could not release the seven bodies until they had confirmation of funeral arrangements. Kevin and Theresa McGovern wanted to ensure that Lorraine and the five children were buried near their family home in Cavan, not in Fermanagh with Arthur. At one point the dispute looked destined for the High Court but eventually it was resolved. On 1 December a joint funeral service, followed by separate burials, was held at the Sacred Heart Church in Omagh. Everyone hoped it would bring closure.

Four hearses carried the coffins to the church on a bitterly cold morning, as children from Caroline's school formed a guard of honour. Arthur's body arrived first in a hearse of its own, followed by Caroline's and Sean's. A third hearse held the slightly smaller white coffins of Bellina and Clodagh. Finally Lorraine and her baby James were brought in the last hearse bearing a floral wreath, saying simply 'Family'.

Inside the church the seven coffins lay side by side and parish priest Monsignor Joseph Donnelly attempted to offer words of hope to the devastated community: 'To lose an entire family unit in one instance is unimaginable. It is devastating for the families immediately connected. It is a loss so total that words fail to describe the immensity of the events . . . The visual impact of what lies before us leaves us in no doubt about the horrible reality. It has also inflicted unbearable suffering and pain on a whole community, especially on the Lammy Crescent community, who were traumatised by what happened.'

The choir of Sacred Heart College sang at the mass. Pupils from St Conor's Primary lined the streets as the coffins were carried from the church by members of both families and placed in the hearses. A few hundred yards down the road, the cortège stopped and, proof that this was no ordinary funeral, the families went their separate ways. The McElhill family returned to Ederney, where Arthur was buried alone, and the McGoverns took Lorraine and her children across the border and laid them to rest in a single grave at Corlough.

Over the weeks up to the funerals, Baxter's team had been sifting through mounds of documents about McElhill and Social Services involvement with the family, trying to put together the puzzle about why he had resorted to mass murder. Baxter was very concerned about the speculation and reports that flooded the papers every day about McElhill's past. He worried about the McElhill and McGovern families, and the effect that these unconfirmed reports were having on them. He decided to wait until after the funerals to try to quell the speculation about the case.

On 3 December 2007, just two days after the family had been buried, he issued a lengthy statement: 'The investigation has been complicated and protracted, due to the difficult crime scene and the need to process a substantial volume of expert analysis. There is much work to be done before a final, definitive account of what happened can be compiled. But it is appropriate at this time to provide an update on the investigation. Police would ask all concerned to appreciate the limits about what can be said at this stage.'

He continued: 'From midday on 13 November 2007,

detectives from the PSNI Serious Crime Branch have been conducting a major investigation into the circumstances surrounding the death of a family who were resident at 4 Lammy Crescent. Following an initial investigation by forensic scientists on the afternoon and early evening of the thirteenth, it became apparent that the circumstances surrounding the fire created the possibility that this was a potential crime. On Wednesday, 14 November, following initial forensic tests at the Forensic Science Laboratory at Carrickfergus, confirmation was received that an accelerant was present within the property. At this point the PSNI commenced a murder inquiry.'

Baxter shifted uneasily. 'In the days which have followed the commencement of the murder investigation, there has been significant media coverage of this horrendous crime. The PSNI are grateful to the media for carrying details of our appeals for information from witnesses and other people with information to come forward to assist the inquiry team. However, some elements of the media have deviated into unhelpful speculation, with the publication of rumour and gossip presented in a sensational and graphic manner. This approach has been unhelpful to the police investigators, who are trying to obtain evidence from witnesses in an untainted environment.'

He went on to confirm that, as a result of the postmortem tests on the bodies of all seven members of the family, it had been established that all were alive before the fire started and died as a consequence of smoke inhalation. 'At this stage police wish to correct some inaccurate and misleading material which has been published. No member of the family was tied up or bound in any manner. The family members were not locked in one room. The bodies of the family members were found in different rooms on the top floor of the dwelling. While it will be the responsibility of a coroner to determine the facts surrounding these seven deaths, police believe it is now appropriate to release the following information: police have established that the fire was started inside the house after accelerant was deposited in the hallway and lounge prior to being ignited. Forensic examination has indicated that the fire was ignited at the base of the stairs. It has also been established that the fire could not have ignited from a source external to the house. Police can confirm that they are not looking for anyone else in connection with the investigation.'

The news that the fire was started at the base of the stairs chilled those who had followed the case: it suggested that McElhill had been adamant that nobody was going to get out that night.

Baxter continued: 'The past three weeks have been a harrowing experience for the dedicated team of police officers working on this investigation, both within the Serious Crime Branch and the local community police in Omagh. Out of the burned wreckage of this family home, there will be many poignant memories of what the public, firefighters, scientists and police encountered in seeking to rescue members of the family, extinguish the flames and subsequently investigate an unimaginable crime. One image may bring some comfort to the wider family circle. At four fifty-four a.m. on the thirteenth of November a 999 call was made to the Fire and Rescue Service from within 4 Lammy Crescent. The investigation team have established that Caroline, at thirteen years of age, had the presence of mind and bravery to seek help from the emergency services to save her family. Caroline was recovered with her telephone in one hand and her rosary beads in the other. This was a young girl, an emblem of innocence, with the courage to seek help, and turning to her faith in the midst of fear and danger. It is my intention at the appropriate time to acknowledge Caroline's actions in seeking help for her family by nominating her for a posthumous award in recognition of her courage.'

He continued: 'It is the fervent hope of the investigation team that last weekend's funerals, followed by the release of this information, which has been briefed personally to the McElhill and McGovern families, will contribute in some way towards a degree of closure in terms of the enormous human tragedy which has unfolded and engulfed them. It will be the responsibility of a coroner to make a fuller determination as to how individual members of the family came to meet their death. It is the police view that further speculation would be unhelpful to the investigation and hurtful to the families.'

The news of Caroline's 999 call and that she had been found with her mobile phone and rosary beads was to become one of the most heartbreaking images of the fire and remains so to this day.

Baxter's statement had quelled rumours that the children were tied up or bound before the fire was lit. But despite his protestations about unhelpful speculation in the media, it appeared that most of what had been reported was far from untrue. In fact the media had revealed just the tip of the iceberg when it came to McElhill and his tangled web of sexual abuse, deceit and fear that would result in the worst familicide Ireland has ever seen.

In the months ahead, Baxter's team would find even more sinister details about McElhill and what he was really up to in the weeks before the fire. For investigators, what initially emerged was a picture of a family who had evidently slipped through the net of the authorities, a family that was far from normal and was ruled by a man living in a seedy world of predatory sex – a man whose desire for young teenage girls had become insatiable. Their probe had taken them back to the beginning.

Arthur McElhill's early years in Fermanagh were unremarkable and not marked by the violence he would later display towards women. There was little that would distinguish him from any other young boy. One of nine children, he was born on 5 October 1971, and was reared in the small townland of Tiermacspirid – three miles outside Ederney in Tyrone. He was known as an obliging and hard-working boy, who turned to manual labour after proving non-academic in school. From his teenage years he developed a problem with drink, which would manifest and unleash an ugly side of his personality that was focused on young girls.

Initially he took work in construction and on farms, but from his teens he was evidently suffering some form of mental turmoil. When he was just seventeen he attended a mental health clinic at Tyrone and Fermanagh Hospital, after a number of suicide attempts. He was assessed as suffering from depression. A month later he was back at the hospital and this time admitted following a further suicide attempt. After six days he was discharged, against medical advice, but continued contact with a mental-health social worker.

Seven months later, in 1989, McElhill was discharged from the service and fell off the radar. By the time he was twenty-one, McElhill had been involved in a terrifying shooting incident when he was driving a car and his passenger was wounded. It appears he took solace in alcohol.

In 1993, aged just twenty-two, he committed his first sexual assault on a sleeping seventeen-year-old. He was caught and brought to court, where he agreed that he would refrain from taking alcohol as part of his probation. But his interest in young teenage girls was not stemmed by the counselling sessions in the hospital's psychosexual clinic. In fact, while he was on probation, he started a sexual relationship with Lorraine, who was only fourteen.

She came from a large family and grew up in the townland of Ardberra near Bawnboy in Cavan. She, too, left school early. A caring child, she had always longed for a big family of her own. When she met McElhill, she was instantly smitten and fell head-over-heels in love with him. However, she was also very aware of his quick temper, and when she found out she was expecting Caroline, she hid the pregnancy from him and her family for eight months for fear of a backlash. Although her parents were deeply disappointed that their daughter had had a child so young – she was only fifteen years and eleven months at the time – they accepted her back to the house after the birth and hoped that, given time, she would get over Arthur, of whom they did not approve.

It was just five months before Caroline's birth that Arthur walked away with a suspended sentence and a one-year custody probation order for the attack on the seventeen-year-old girl. His victim was devastated by the sentence. Later, on a BBC *Spotlight* documentary about the fire, she said that she was in no doubt about Arthur McElhill's violent streak.

She had been asleep in her bedroom on a Sunday morning in January 1993 when McElhill broke in: 'I was awoken with a person crawling up the bed. The duvet was wrapped all around me and he seemed to be under it. That is when the attack took place. He continually punched away the whole time. I had such difficulty in breathing. I was calling out for help but it continued on and on. I thought, If I don't get screaming one more time, this is it. I am going to be a goner. I didn't know if he was going to rape me when I was alive or dead. He was just like an animal – a frenzied animal. Just, you know – the strength of his punches. Bam, bam, into your face. I didn't think I would survive it, to be honest.'

McElhill had fled the house when a relative came to the victim's rescue, but when he was arrested, he denied everything. Hours before he had broken into the seventeen-year-old's room, he had been discovered lurking in the bedroom of two sleeping teenage girls. He was visiting the house at the time and had gone missing. When the girls' father went to look for him, he found him standing over his sleeping daughters. Furious, he threw McElhill out of the house.

After the court case, McElhill went back to live with his parents, and Lorraine stayed at home with hers, but her attraction to McElhill never waned. At one point she worked at the four-star Slieve Russell Hotel at nearby Ballyconnell, but any hopes her family had that she would get on with her life without him were dashed when, with just weeks to go before her eighteenth birthday, she left and moved to Omagh to be near him. She moved in with his sister and he stayed with her while still basing himself, for the sake of the authorities, at his parents' home.

Less than eight weeks after the couple were reunited, Arthur McElhill broke into a caravan where he subjected another seventeen-year-old girl to a horrific assault.

His second victim had been sleeping in a caravan when she was attacked, in September 1996. She also spoke to *Spotlight* and gave further chilling details of the exact nature of the attack: 'I woke up to find someone had come into the caravan and I was faced with a fairly physical and brutal attack. It is important people understand what he was like. I was as terrified as ever I have been. I didn't know how things were going to go. I remember just feeling physically helpless, and as strong and fit as I was, I couldn't do anything about it. I have never been as terrified. I didn't know if I was going to live through it or what was going to happen. At one point he stood up to take up his trousers and I managed to strike him and he got frightened. I was a child and absolutely terrified.'

As she grappled with McElhill, someone heard the commotion and came to her rescue, but later she had to go to court and face him again. 'At the time I didn't want to go and struggled for a bit with it. I wanted everyone who knew about it to go away. I wanted to forget about it and hide from it. I was a child and I didn't understand at the time what effect it would have on me in later life. But the one thing that motivated me to follow it through was so it couldn't happen to anyone else.'

The case took two years to get to court but McElhill was given a three-year prison sentence, of which he served half.

By the time Lorraine moved to Lammy Crescent, Arthur was telling social workers that he could identify his own risk factors, which included alcohol, sexual talk among males and emotional stress. He was noted in prison as being 'at high risk of committing sexual offences again'. Child protection case conferences had been held in respect of young Caroline, and her name was placed on the register under the category of 'Potential Sexual Abuse'. Neighbours on the estate had no idea that the single mum pregnant with her second child was waiting patiently for the day that her sex-offender lover could move in with her.

Lorraine was adamant that she and Arthur would be together and the couple started working with Social Services to come to an agreement about how he would move in with her and Caroline. When Sean was born in 2000, it was decided that there was no need for a core group to meet in respect of child-protection matters for the infant. In June 2000 a case conference was held about the family, and a psychologist at Erne House, working with McElhill, was of the view that his abuse of alcohol had diminished and that in light of his offending he was a risk only to older teenage girls, not to children. The psychologist said he would continue working with McElhill but suggested that further work be done with Lorraine to train her to act as a protector for her children.

McElhill said he wanted to move in with Lorraine and his children but didn't know whether or not he was permitted to do so. By the following November, he notified the PSNI and the probation service that he was moving to Lammy Crescent.

After Bellina was born in 2003, Lorraine was diagnosed with post-natal depression and prescribed medication until she fell pregnant with Clodagh. Their fourth child was born in April 2006, followed quickly by James. Between 2000 and 2007 Baxter's team had noted, during their investigation into the fire, that there was no Social Services involvement with the family, and while health visitors had continued to see them, they did not see or report anything untoward.

In Northern Ireland, as the investigation continued, calls were made for an independent review of agency involvement with the couple and their children. It was ordered in January 2008, two months after the fire, by the Department of Health, Social Services and Public Safety, and was to be headed by Henry Toner QC. The work of the review panel was to consider the quality of the professional work of the various agencies involved with the couple and their children, particularly in the area of child protection, arising from the criminal offences previously committed by McElhill. Its findings would be damning.

At the same time the PSNI was putting together the case

that would form the inquest into the family's deaths, and the team found themselves concentrating on what had happened during 2007. It showed that McElhill was far from the 'low risk' offender that Social Services had deemed him. Police were piecing together a picture of how McElhill had been building up to a crescendo of sexual abuse that would put at risk the core of his world.

Phone records showed intense contact between McElhill and two teenage girls in the four months before the fire. Officers discovered that he had befriended the teenagers and suspected that he was having sex with one of them. The girl worked for the couple as a babysitter and had recently been staying at the house. She was interviewed shortly after the fire. At that time she said that McElhill and Lorraine were having no problems in their relationship, that he was not drinking and that she was not in a sexual relationship with him. By August 2008, as the investigation intensified, she changed her story and admitted having sex with him and of being in intense mobile phone contact with him in the days before his death.

The girl admitted to officers that she had started her relationship with him just four months before the fire. She said they sometimes had sex in a bedroom while Lorraine was downstairs, unaware of what was going on. Officers suspected otherwise – that Lorraine had known about it. The girl admitted that they had had sex up to ten times in the house during the weeks leading up to the blaze. It had begun after McElhill brought her upstairs to show her his computer at some point during that July. On the first occasion he kissed her, but a month later he had used the same ruse to have sex with her. He had locked the bedroom door from the inside with a key, then pulled the curtains. She insisted to investigators that the sex had been consensual.

A friend of McElhill told investigators that Arthur had said the girl reminded him of Lorraine when she was that age. At the same time he was also trying to groom another teenager, with obscene text messages and phone calls begging her for sex. He had got her phone number from a friend and begun sending the texts and making the calls in the weeks prior to the blaze. She told officers that in one call, McElhill had asked her to go for a drive with him and some friends. He told her they could 'make love on the back seat' and he claimed he was just twenty.

Officers discovered that he had become stressed and was drinking heavily as a result. A third teenager, a friend of Caroline, was a runaway and under the care of Social Services. On and off over a three-month period, she regularly slept at Lammy Crescent and was often returned there by her family support worker – an element of her care that was strongly criticised in the Toner Report. But by August, the situation between the couple and the teenager's mother had become fraught. The girl was refusing to come home and Social Services were looking into McElhill's background.

In the meantime, he was conducting a sexual relationship with his babysitter and had started using his son Sean's Bebo site to contact other young girls. In one online conversation with a twelve-year-old girl he asked if Caroline had a boyfriend. Officers also suspected that at this time he was beating Lorraine regularly. Surrounded by teenage girls and living out his sexual fantasies with one of them, he was spiralling out of control.

In September 2007, when the mother of Caroline's runaway friend found out that McElhill had a history of attacking teenagers, she went to the house and demanded her daughter come home. A social worker was called and said she would speak to the teenager. That week McElhill went to see his GP, Dr Michelle Mellotte. She had been his doctor since 1993 and was also the family GP. He told her he was really down and depressed and finding things difficult. He complained about being overweight and said he found the workload at home difficult: Lorraine was 'unnecessarily shouting at the children'. When the doctor probed about his feelings, he said he had no suicidal thoughts and she prescribed anti-depressants. She made an appointment for him later in October but he failed to attend.

At the family inquest, the doctor described how his medical records showed that he had suffered from depression in the 1980s when he tried to crash his car into a wall after a friend died: 'He had been in a distressed state when he was hospitalised but he calmed down quite quickly and was discharged. I discovered in his medical records that he had been depressed then, and in October 1997, but was not suicidal when I saw him and he'd no recent changes to his treatment.' She said she had met him later by chance outside her surgery but that he had seemed in good form. 'I had prescribed him anti-depressants but I cannot say how many he took, if he took any at all. He had not complied with instructions on other occasions. He did not get a second prescription from me. I had asked him if he'd had suicidal thoughts, if he had trouble with sleep, appetite, interest in things, whether he thought sometimes that life was not worth living or if he had plans for his death or the death of others. I asked him if he felt anger or depression towards himself or other people. He gave me negative answers to all those questions.'

Just over a week later, when the mother of the runaway returned to Lammy Crescent, yet again demanding her daughter come home and accusing McElhill of being a sex offender, the police were called. Over a dispatch, an officer who monitored sex offenders happened to hear Arthur's name. He informed officers at the scene about McElhill's offending history and they contacted Social Services. It took another day for the child to be removed from the house by social workers.

At home, tensions grew and the rows between Arthur and Lorraine intensified. Many believe she at least suspected he was having sex with their babysitter.

On 14 October, a month before her tragic death, Caroline contacted the PSNI in a distressed state about a row between her parents. She gave her name and address, and police officers went and talked to Lorraine, who said that Caroline had overreacted and the row was over. She said Arthur and the children had gone to bed. The officers left.

The last time the babysitter admitted to officers that she had had sex with McElhill was three weeks before the fire. Two days before that fateful night, McElhill exchanged 154 text messages with her and the other sixteen-year-old, and spent an hour-and-a-half talking to them on the phone. On the day before the blaze, he exchanged twenty-one messages with the girl, and had thirty-four phone conversations with the babysitter, lasting two hours and thirty-one minutes. She refused to give officers details of the conversations but told them she was minding the children that night, as Arthur and Lorraine had attended a car auction, where they were said to be in good spirits.

In June 2008, the Toner Report was published and its findings sent shockwaves across the Northern Ireland care system. It was littered with references to failures within it. Reports had not been presented, minutes had not been written up, there has been no liaison between agencies, and when the family file was reopened in 2007, after Caroline's friend had stayed at the house, vital information about McElhill's sexual past was not included. The Report detailed how in 2001, when McElhill ceased to be the subject of a probation order, he was assessed as being of medium risk to the public. Three years later, an area sex-offender risk-management committee review had reassessed him as low risk. Later it emerged that social workers dealing with the family were unaware of his convictions, even though the information was on their own records. Lack of resources was found to be a fundamental problem and young, inexperienced social workers had been left to make crucial decisions with neither support nor key information.

The Report painted a picture of Lorraine McGovern as the classic victim of an abuser and of domestic violence. It detailed how she was prescribed medication for post-natal depression after the birth of Bellina, but went on to have two more children in quick succession. Burdened by the demands of a large family of young children and infatuated by the man who ruled her, she appears to have helped protect McElhill by failing to attend meetings with the health professional who was meant to monitor her role as protector. The Toner Report also found that she had objected to her partner's past offences being raised in relation to the visiting children. Among the findings in the Report was the revelation that, although the police officers involved had told the local health trust of Caroline's call about her parents' row, no social worker had visited.

Northern Ireland Children's Commissioner Patricia Lewsley said the repeated failure to act on the warning signs in the family was horrifying: nothing had been done for the children. 'It is clear from this report that agencies were not talking to each other, individuals' concerns were not listened to.' Stormont's Health Minister Michael McGimpsey, who had

201

commissioned the review, directed the chief Social Services officer to ensure all recommendations were fully implemented.

In the meantime, Baxter's team had completed their investigation for the coroner, and in December 2009, the McElhill and McGovern families met for the final chapter in the tragedy.

For most who gathered in the courtroom and listened to the evidence of what happened on the night of the fire, the dreadful scenes inside the burned-out house, the details of McElhill's relationship with his babysitter and attempts to lure other young girls into his web, one voice rang out stronger than any other. It was the taped recording of Caroline's gasps of terror. It will forever haunt those who heard it. The six-minute recording was unquestionably the most traumatic of all the evidence because it showed the full horror of what happened inside 4 Lammy Crescent that night.

As the flames and black smoke consumed her home, the petrified child had somehow located a mobile phone and dialled 999. When an operator answered she screamed, 'Help me!' and 'I'm burning . . . run!' Muffled screams for help could be heard in the background from other family members. Then Caroline spoke again, only partially coherent now: 'He's k— us.' Gasps, believed to be young Caroline's dying breaths, concluded the call.

A phonetics expert had been asked by police to decipher the missing syllables after the 'k' sound but was unable to do so. Most drew their own conclusions.

Detective Chief Inspector Derek Scott told the inquest that McElhill was a depressive with a history of suicide attempts: he had been capable of starting the fire and exercising control over his family. He said that McElhill was aware that his previous sex offences were being 'talked about'. When Scott was asked if it might be normal for a family with two young children to have bottles of milk packed in a bag, he said no: 'I don't think it was for one night. It would be inconceivable that they would need so much milk.'

After four days of harrowing evidence, Coroner Suzanne Anderson said: 'I'm satisfied, on the balance of probabilities, that Arthur McElhill and Lorraine McGovern had been up all night and that she was about to leave, taking with her at least some of her children, when the fire was started by Arthur McElhill.' She added that she had not been able to prove conclusively that McElhill had intended to commit suicide. She noted that his private life was 'in turmoil' and that he knew his sexual relationship with an underage girl would have meant certain imprisonment, had it become known.

In a statement issued through their solicitor, McElhill's parents, Charles and Patricia, whose family had consistently protested Arthur's innocence, said they would remember a 'happy family'. 'The events of the last two years have devastated and shattered our lives beyond belief. Our pain is immeasurable and it will endure for the rest of our lives. We love and miss Arthur, Lorraine and our grandchildren every day.'

Lorraine's family and her parents, Theresa and Kevin, said they hoped the proceedings would bring them closure. They paid tribute to the firefighters and emergency services who had battled in vain to try to save the family, and to the people of Omagh who had offered them comfort and support.

To this day Norman Baxter, now retired, does not believe there was any evidence that McEhill was going to do what he did that night at Lammy Crescent. He says the couple had started to buy Christmas presents for their children, which were still in the boot of the car when they perished. But he does admit that McElhill was out of control and a master of deception. In a local newspaper, he wrote:

> Northern Irish society must confront the reality that
> people like Arthur McElhill live, work and socialise in
> their midst. They look normal, act normal and remain
> below the radar of law enforcement until they are
> detected offending. The problem is, how can children
> and young people be protected from an unidentified
> 'enemy' lurking in the guise of family members, youth
> workers, church officials and a range of other roles that
> interact with young people? The conclusion of the
> inquest was soon followed by an array of politicians and
> representatives of interest groups who all had a view on
> who to blame and the failures of statutory agencies.
> The police and social workers became easy prey for
> these commentators, who have the privilege of having
> no responsibility for the delivery of public services
> within an ever-expanding workload and diminishing
> resources.
>
> It is easy to criticise those in the front line of service
> delivery from the comfort of a detached responsibility.
> 'How could this happen?' has been the clarion call.
> Someone must be to blame. There must be failures.
> There was even a sombre sound bite that society had
> failed Lorraine McGovern and her children. Today we
> live within the culture of blame – someone always has to
> be to blame. Of course someone was to blame. Arthur
> McElhill was to blame . . .
>
> Could the tragedy at Lammy Crescent have been
> prevented? The mandate seekers seem to think so, but
> the real answer is not that easy to determine. Society
> cannot protect everyone from the actions of others,

especially those who are disturbed. When I was growing up in the hinterland of Omagh, local people spoke of a family who had lived in a neighbouring townland in an earlier generation. One day the family were found dead – mother and children slain by the father, who then took his own life. How could any man kill his children and their mother? It couldn't be true, it couldn't happen. I reasoned the way young people do.

It is widely recognised that the most dangerous time for a woman in an abusive relationship is when she tries to leave. That is when she is most likely to be murdered. But Lorraine McGovern could never have dreamed, when she packed her baby's bottles, that she would unleash an anger in McElhill she had never before seen, which would ensure that nobody in that house would live to see daylight.

9

BALLYCOTTON'S DARKEST DAY
The Butler Tragedy

In Dublin, newsrooms were busy with the constant barrage of bad news flowing in on the economic front. Tuesday, 16 November 2010, was a bleak day and the forecast couldn't have been blacker for Ireland. A budget was due, and it was set to be the worst ever. Anglo Irish Bank had crippled the country, Bank of Ireland and AIB shares were tumbling and it was rumoured that the country might have to be bailed out by the International Monetary Fund. Taoiseach Brian Cowen was denying it and sought to bring calm to the growing speculation that Ireland had indeed gone broke. The crippling lows of the economic bust seemed to hold an uncomfortable mirror to the once-dizzying heights of the boom that had defined Ireland just a few short years ago.

Just as it seemed that things couldn't get any worse, a story broke in Cork. There had been a car crash in a remote East

Cork village that morning and two small children had later been found dead in a house. Gardaí were not looking for anyone in relation to their deaths. Officially, news sites were contained with their reporting, but local correspondents and photographers were already on their way to the scene of what they had been informed was a horrific murder-suicide, involving two small girls and a recently unemployed father who, it appeared, had doused himself in petrol and crashed his car headlong into a wall.

The father in question was John Butler from Ballycotton in County Cork and, by all accounts, he had embarked on his murderous spree after his wife had left for work. The fact that John Butler had been a construction worker rang alarm bells. Was this the face of Ireland's economic collapse, and would John Butler, whoever he was, be the poster boy of the greed that had engulfed and then destroyed a nation? And, more importantly, could things really have got so bad?

As reporters were dispatched from Dublin to the south-east, the news desk phones began to light up again. Another family had been found dead in Limerick. Two children, one only five months old, had been stabbed to death in their beds and two adults were discovered with similar wounds in a room downstairs in a neat council house. Teams of officers were combing the country for a suspect who had gone missing before the bodies had been discovered. News editors rechecked the wires to make sure there was no mistake, then glanced around their newsrooms and, for the second time that day, sent teams to cover the rarest phenomenon of all: the so-called family wipe-out or 'annihilation'.

In both areas of the country, competent detectives and those in charge of the investigation were happy that they had things under control and did not require the help of the National Bureau of Criminal Investigation, the specialist team from Dublin that is regularly brought in to assist local gardaí when murders occur.

As speculation grew that the crimes might be linked, given the coincidence of two such incidents on the same day, officers heading the investigations knew from early on that two separate tragedies had simply collided in time.

By evening, a man was in custody in Limerick, in connection with the murders of Sarah Hines, aged twenty-five, her son Reece, who was three, her five-month-old daughter Amy, and Sarah's friend Alicia Brough, all of whom had all been found in the Hazelgrove estate. (John Geary, a former partner of Sarah's, is currently before the courts charged with the four murders. He was arrested in a bar in Kilkee, on a drinking binge. Earlier, he had calmly eaten a curry while the bodies lay in the house.)

In Cork, though, a different scenario was unfolding and a mother was facing a lifetime of questions and the stark realisation that her babies had been killed by their own flesh and blood.

For Una O'Riordan, it had been a childhood of sea stories, days on the long sandy beaches and the odd trip on one of the many fishing boats her family took out every day to catch hauls of cod, mackerel and pollack.

The O'Riordans had long been part of the maritime tapestry that made up the little village of Ballycotton, located twenty-five miles from Cork and sandwiched between Shanagarry and Churchtown. Throughout her childhood, Una would regularly gaze across the bay and along the coast that leads to Capel Island, or out over the expanse of blue-grey water that stretches as far as the eye can see. While her summers were long and carefree, the winters were bitter and bracing, as the cold wind blew in from the Irish Sea and cut through the narrow, winding streets of the village.

Every Sunday she would dress up with the rest of her family and they would make their way to mass, where they prayed that the uncles, cousins and parents who went to sea every day would be safe. On occasion they dressed in black and mourned those who had been taken by the waves.

After leaving school Una went on to university and eventually landed a post in the Revenue Department in Cork. As a civil servant, she could make her way up the grades and was guaranteed a job for life and a pension. She moved into the city. There she met John Butler, a crane operator from Cobh and an acclaimed sportsman. He worked at Irish Steel, high above Haulbowline harbour, until the company closed in 2001. He, like many others, was left jobless. He was a six-footer and came from a large and very close family. He was a footballer, a local GAA star acclaimed for his work on the pitch. In his free time, he put all his efforts into his sporting prowess.

By then the couple had married and, with John's redundancy package, they opted to make a life-changing decision. Una knew she wanted children and to bring them up close to her own tight-knit family, with the support she would need if she was to continue her career. She wasn't the first who had fled the nest only to be drawn back to the comfort of the little fishing village. To the outsider, Ballycotton might be nothing more than a mish-mash of small pubs, corner shops, a school – blink, and you'd miss it. Keep going, and you land in the sea. But it's always been a place that has drawn its children home.

The couple bought a site and started to build a bungalow, which they hoped would serve them for life. Around it they constructed outhouses, where John could forge his own business in construction and general handyman jobs. He bought equipment that would set him up to develop a thriving industry from home. Any money he brought in would supplement Una's salary.

Ballycotton is notoriously clannish but Una's large, extended family welcomed John as one of their own and helped him find work. He was kept busy during the boom, working with various builders on one-off houses and extensions, while Una made the daily sixty-mile round trek to Cork.

The couple rarely went out and were not big drinkers. John was quiet and preferred to stay at home, rather than hang around bars drinking with fishermen.

They settled into their bungalow, and while John picked up regular work, he harboured no ambitions to become a private developer, like many of his peers. He preferred instead to earn a wage for his labour during an honest day's work.

Una managed the household budgets and when, in 2004, the couple celebrated the birth of their first child, Zoë, she knew she would be returning to work. Zoë was a beautiful baby and appeared to make their life complete. After three years, Una reckoned it was time for another child and soon became pregnant with Ella.

Una was renowned for being excellent at her job and, from the outside, appeared adept at juggling that aspect of her life with motherhood. But she was realistic, too, and knew that she was the family breadwinner: her guaranteed salary was vital to pay the household bills and loans until such a time that John's business took off.

When Ella was born, it would have taken Zoë a little time to adjust to the demands a baby put on her parents. But life was good, save for the occasions when John became low and couldn't pull himself out of bed to find work. When he had a job, the couple employed a childminder, a local girl, who was like a second mother to the girls. When John was at home, he looked after the children.

A year before the tragic events of November 2010, John disappeared. After a build-up of depression, he walked out of the door, leaving his wallet behind. Una was so worried about him she contacted the gardaí, but within twenty-four hours he had returned of his own volition. It was the one and only time John Butler had come to the attention of the gardaí.

In the months leading up to his shocking actions in 2010, John was besieged with depression and attended a doctor who prescribed him an anti-depressant, which it was hoped would keep his moods steady and help chemically to balance his brain.

He was out of work and minding the children, a very hands-on father who, despite his condition, was fully competent when it came to Zoë and Ella. Together they had a little routine, which involved John and Ella dropping Zoë to school, then returning to collect her in the afternoon. On nice days they would go to the beach or play in the garden. They would regularly drop in on relatives as they waited for Una to come home from work.

On the morning of 16 November, life was pretty normal in the Butler household. Day broke grey and cold, and a mist hung over Ballycotton Bay. John seemed down, but that was nothing unusual. The girls were up and about in their pyjamas as Una dressed for work. John was up too. He put some bread in the toaster as the girls settled down in front of the television to watch their favourite show, before they had to dress and make the short drive to Zoë's school.

Although John didn't appear any more out of sorts than

was usual, recently Una's anxiety about his declining moods had been building, and she suspected that he had stopped taking his medication. When she arrived in work shortly after 8 a.m., she phoned his mobile to make sure they were ready and headed for school. When he didn't answer, she continued phoning, but to no avail. She called one of his sisters and asked her to phone him to see if there was anything she could do to cheer him. Still he didn't pick up Una's increasingly frantic calls.

For the next hour Una continued to worry about why John wasn't answering her calls, and as rising panic gripped her, she decided to leave work for the day and drive home to make sure all was well. She would soon learn that everything was far from well. Tuesday, 16 November 2010, would be etched in her mind for the rest of her life as the blackest day she would ever know.

For the community of Ballycotton, life had continued as normal throughout the morning. The children had arrived at Star of the Sea School on the village main street, and one by one made their way to their desks. In the first classroom, one seat was vacant, but it wasn't unusual for a child to be out sick for a day or two at this time of year and no one paid any heed.

Shortly before ten a.m. everything would change in that pretty corner of Ireland. When officers were called to the scene of an accident at a notorious bad bend on the way from Shanagarry into Ballycotton, they immediately knew that this was no ordinary crash. The car, a Toyota, had exploded on impact. It had hit a wall so hard it had stood on its end in a burning inferno. Officers were told the vehicle belonged to John Butler, who should have been minding his two children. Firefighters brought the blaze under control and investigators searched the wreckage to see how many bodies were inside. Those who stood on the roadside that day dreaded to hear that two little bodies had been strapped into the back.

Gardaí, under veteran Superintendent Flor Horan of Midleton Garda Station, knew even as the fire raged that this had been suicide: Butler would have known the road so well that he couldn't possibly have ploughed straight into the ditch unless he had fallen asleep, but the time of day made that virtually impossible. Witnesses were able to tell them that the car had turned into a fireball the minute it had hit the ditch. That, and the level of the blaze, immediately aroused suspicions that an accelerant had been present.

As soon as the fire was brought under control, it was discovered that only one body lay in the car – in the driver's seat. Sisters of Una, who had been alerted to what had happened, immediately made their way to the Butlers' bungalow to check on the children. At that stage they knew that Zoë wasn't in school, and now that it had been confirmed she and Ella were not in the car, they may have felt some relief. But if they did, it was short-lived. At the house they broke a window to get inside and there, in the front sitting room, they found the bodies of Zoë and Ella.

While officers sealed off the crash scene, other members of Horan's team made their way to the house, which was also sealed off. But there was more to do. A panicked Una was on her way back to Ballycotton, and Horan was adamant that she would not drive straight into the crash scene where her husband still lay in the mangled mess of his red car. He deployed a squad to stop her en route, and just outside Cloyne, they pulled her in and gently broke the appalling news to her.

In what must have been the surreal days that followed, a media mob descended on Ballycotton, which was utterly stunned by the circumstances it found itself thrown into: it was making headline news for the most tragic of reasons.

When the bodies were released, Una decided to bring all

three home to the family bungalow where John's remains lay between those of his two little girls. Journalists were issued with the standard appeal for privacy, but things turned sour as they stood out among the small and tight-knit populace of the fishing village. There were minor incidents: one news team was run out of a local bar, two photographers were threatened and many vented their disgust with those who were reporting on John Butler's crime.

By Thursday afternoon John Butler's body was removed to Cobh Cathedral. On its journey, a group of mourners stopped at the spot where he had crashed. Una Butler laid a single red rose for her husband.

The following morning she was faced with the enormous task of burying her little girls. The Star of the Sea Church is not used to such crowds. Located high on a hill overlooking the bay, it has served the community for generations, but that cold Friday morning it was packed as never before. Speakers were hung on the railings outside to accommodate the hundreds of mourners who had come from miles around to pay their respects to the children.

The crunch of gravel from the road below signalled the arrival of the hearse. The sight of the small coffins caused a collective gasp, as those who had busied themselves all week making sandwiches and pots of tea saw for the first time the stark effect of the unbelievable tragedy that had unfolded among them.

Schoolfriends formed a guard of honour for Zoë and Ella as they were carried into the same church where they had been brought by their parents every Sunday, where they had been christened and where Zoë had looked forward to making her First Holy Communion along with her classmates.

Mourners who hadn't personally known the children learned a bit about the sisters that day: about Ella, the mischievous two-year-old, who had locked herself into a wardrobe, which had had to be dismantled. She loved to dance and couldn't be persuaded to leave the floor at a recent Hallowe'en party. Zoë was caring and outgoing; she loved judo and shoes. Father Aidan Crowley said he usually saw the girls at the church for nine-thirty a.m. mass on Sunday with their parents.

One little tale was told that made John Butler's actions all the more inexplicable. It was a simple story about sunscreen and a bright day that could have played out anywhere in Ireland. A father calls his daughters over to him as they play on the pier. He is worried that, although it is cold, the sun might burn them. He gently applies sunscreen to their faces to protect them. As the congregation listened to the description of a scene that had so recently played out, in which a father's hands had shown such care, the new reality – that those same hands had been used, just a few short weeks later, to end those lives – seemed all the more difficult to comprehend.

Wiping tears from her eyes, one weather-beaten woman turned to the stranger beside her and whispered, 'It's like I'm having a dream and I'm going to wake up . . . He loved those girls. He couldn't have done this.'

But he had, and throughout the week, the facts of what had happened on that dreadful morning slowly emerged as Superintendent Horan's team painstakingly pieced together every detail of Butler's actions.

In the incident room, it had been established that on Tuesday morning, after making them breakfast, Butler had strangled his children, first Zoë, then Ella. Then he had grabbed his keys and walked out of his well-kept bungalow, his home of ten years, leaving his mobile phone on the hall table. Inexplicably, he had locked the door.

He had got into his car and driven, past the spot where he

would later perish, to a petrol station and convenience store. There he had filled a jerry-can with twenty euros' worth of petrol. Staff who served him would later tell police that he appeared agitated. He placed the canister on the passenger seat and drove off. Twenty minutes later his Toyota exploded into the fireball.

While officers had pieced together most of the details of what had happened, they did not know where Butler had gone between the petrol station and the crash site. They suspected he had driven to one of the many isolated beaches that dot the area, but they needed witnesses to find out exactly where he had been, to see if he had left any clues there or perhaps a note to explain his actions.

Toxicology results were vital to the investigation that Horan was putting together for the coroner, and Butler's full medical history had been requested.

The following morning a huge crowd gathered at Cobh's St Coman's Cathedral for his funeral mass, where mourners were told he was a 'beloved' husband and father, who was generous, energetic, talented and hard-working. His coffin was draped with the Cobh GAA Club flag. His mother Kitty was supported by sons Chris, Paul and Pat, daughters Marie, Kathryn and Brid, and their extended families. Una also attended the ceremony with members of her extended family. She arrived separately from the official funeral party but stood in solidarity with them in the cathedral.

Father John McCarthy, who officiated at the mass, said that the previous Tuesday will be 'for ever sealed into the memory' of the people of Cork. 'We ask ourselves, can this be happening? It is inconceivable that we are here. There are so many unanswered questions . . . We are filled with despair . . . So many of us are lost for words. There are no words.'

But he told mourners to remember John as a committed family man, who loved Una and doted on his girls. He described how he had showered his nieces and nephews with presents, buying the biggest toys for them. 'This is the John that the Butler family will remember,' he said. He prayed that God would 'forgive John his sins and grant him a place of happiness, light and peace'.

'This is all we can do at a time like this,' he told mourners. 'For both the Butler and O'Riordan families, we are here for you. We pray for healing and forgiveness for John in these most difficult of circumstances, and our continued prayers and love in the days and months ahead.'

Outside, as his family gathered to bring him for cremation, Una placed a single red rose on John's coffin. It was a sign of her love and devotion to the man who had, in a very real sense, ended her life.

On the Sunday, officers appealed at masses in the East Cork area for anyone who had information about Butler's whereabouts during the missing twenty-minute period.

Within days a witness told gardaí that they had seen Butler driving towards a lonely beach known as Ard Na Hench near Shanagarry, where it is now believed he doused his car and himself in petrol before the crash. In the weeks that followed, it was revealed that the investigation team had also discovered stashes of his anti-depressant medication around his home.

Despite the tragedy, the Butler and O'Riordan families have remained united. Una has been praised for her bravery and strength over the dreadful months that have followed. An inquest is likely to be held towards the middle of 2011. It is expected that any explanations given for John Butler's actions will have more to do with his state of mind and less to do with the state of the Irish economy at the time.

CONCLUSION

Explaining the Inexplicable

To a jury in Greece, John Hogan was insane when he jumped from a balcony at a holiday resort taking his six-year-old son Liam and two-year-old daughter Mia with him. Incredibly the tiler survived the fifty-foot fall. So, too, did little Mia – but her brother died instantly from the horrific head injuries he sustained when he hit the ground.

Throughout his trial Hogan, the son of Irish immigrants to Bristol in the UK, insisted that he felt 'no guilt' about Liam's death because the real him had not done it. He said he remembered nothing about what he referred to as 'the accident'.

The 'balcony leap case' has caused huge controversy in the UK, where an inquest into Liam's death was quashed when the High Court ruled that the coroner, Paul Forrest, had not taken into account Hogan's state of mind when he returned a verdict of 'unlawful killing' in relation to the child's death. Hogan has since returned to the UK, after three years in a Greek psychiatric hospital. He is now living as a free man.

The case fits classically into what experts have recognised as the largely male phenomenon of familicide, which is the murder of an entire family by a family member. In the US, Professor Jack Levin, a leading expert in the field from Northeastern University in Boston, has coined the phrase 'family annihilators'. He has profiled them as middle-aged men, who are good providers, and seen as dedicated husbands and devoted fathers. But they tend to be isolated individuals who suffer from feelings of inadequacy. He states that when they suffer a 'catastrophic loss', which is usually financial or a relationship, they feel an overwhelming sense of powerlessness. In revenge they turn on their wife and children. John Hogan had become depressed: he suspected his wife, Natasha, of infidelity and believed she was about to leave him. He had evidently developed a strong sense of ownership of his children. When he plunged from the sun-drenched balcony, he was a father driven mad who, in his twisted mind, believed he was taking his children with him to a better place.

Or so we are led to understand.

As with all instances of familicide and murder-suicide – which is the murder of one or more people followed by the suicide of the killer within a week – it is easy for academics, those who study psychology, and experts in such cases to try to categorise such catastrophes in an effort to make sense of the incomprehensible. But while familicidal killers often share certain characteristics, their actions are the result of many different circumstances, relationships, emotions and motives.

Hogan's crime, or attempted crime, was not strictly familicide. Nor was it filicide, the act of killing one's own son or daughter, then committing suicide. So, Hogan doesn't fall into any textbook definition. His decision to jump with his children, leaving his wife packing suitcases, rules him out of familicide. However, there is no doubt that he intended to kill himself and his children. That he and Mia survived further complicates his categorisation.

However, from digging deeper into his background and the circumstances that led to his actions, it is easy to see that he shared certain emotions and traits with others who have carried out some of the most dreadful cases known of 'family annihilation'. Hogan's case is of particular interest for a number of reasons, namely his survival and the controversy caused in his native UK and its law courts by the Greek court's declaration of his insanity.

John Hogan may still be suffering from his injuries, but he lived to tell the tale of what went through his mind when he decided on the course of action he took. But, like others who have survived whatever primeval urge spurred them on to kill or attempt to end their own lives, he has done so behind the closed doors of psychiatric institutions to sympathetic counsellors.

In the courtroom, where the tale of a warring couple emerged, it was Hogan's voice that was heard, through his psychiatrist Dr Ioannis Nestoros, more prominently than any other. Nestoros said his client was suffering from an 'earthquake' of psychosis as a result of his wife telling him she was leaving him. While he had waited for his trial, Hogan had told his psychiatrist about his difficult childhood in Bristol, growing up in an overcrowded home with his mother, Josephine, father, John senior, and six siblings. He told both Nestoros and Dr Markos Skondras that he never heard his parents say they loved him and that he, as head of the family after his father's death, felt responsible for the suicides of two of his brothers, Paul and Stephen.

At the beginning of his relationship with Natasha, he had

developed agoraphobia and begun suffering panic attacks. With the birth of his son Liam, in May 2000, he had felt better. Within two years the couple were married, and after another two years Mia was born. A month later, Hogan had received the devastating news that his brother Paul had set fire to the family home, then thrown himself off a nearby suspension bridge, killing himself. He told his Greek medical team that this had had a profound effect on him and he felt like the one 'left behind'. As the months wore on, Hogan became increasingly unhinged and concentrated on his relationship with Natasha, which he felt was slipping away from him. When he found flirtatious emails between her and an old friend, he exploded. In February 2006 the couple had decided to take a make-it-or-break-it holiday in Greece.

On the day they arrived, they were given a room on the Petra Mare Hotel's top floor, instead of the ground-floor apartment they had booked. By day four Natasha was very concerned about her husband's behaviour. He demanded continuously to know whether or not she was going to leave him. He would later tell his psychiatrists that the death of his brothers, particularly Paul, was on his mind. He also said: 'I couldn't bear the thought that I would be left alone, that I would come in from work and not see my kids.' Finally, unable to take another row, Natasha began to pack her bags.

A year and a half later she would tell a court: 'I started rearranging the cases and he was shouting at me. He stared at me, a crazed look, and started shouting, "My packing is crap. John's packing is crap." I had my back to him. Then I turned around and no one was there. I heard a woman scream . . . He did not need to try and kill my children. He did not need to take my children . . . I believe the suicides in his family may have contributed to his desire to commit suicide. That was why he needed to try and kill himself, but he should not have tried to take my children . . . It was a selfish love.'

Dr Nestoros told the court: 'It was not his intention to harm the children. He thought he would take them by the hand and walk them to Heaven. When he attempted suicide, he thought his son was in Paradise and that he was going to join him to protect him. If his wife had not told him that she was going to divorce him then this wouldn't have happened. It wasn't particularly intelligent of her to say things at this time.'

The court accepted Hogan's defence that he was in the grip of an overwhelming psychotic episode when he threw his son Liam over the fourth floor balcony of the family's holiday hotel, before leaping with his two-year-old daughter in his arms. His wife contends that he put up a sterling performance to get away with murder. Certainly, some experts would be more inclined to agree with her than with his defence team.

Dr Chris Milroy, who spent twenty years working as a forensic pathologist at the University of Sheffield and is now based in Canada, is one of the few people who have studied murder-suicides and familicides extensively. After years of research he says that most perpetrators who survive almost always plead insanity, but there is little evidence to suggest they have any psychiatric problems. 'It is very difficult to say for certain, but it appears that most of these people, if they came before the courts – most if not all – would have understood exactly what they had done. They would not be insane. Most of them would not have had any known psychiatric problems in the past. I had a case of a man who separated from his wife. They had a child together and there were some issues over custody. He killed the child and he wrote a suicide note or told other people, "If I can't have her, the bitch can't have her." That is a very similar case to that of Chris Crowley. That was something that happened in anger and I think that is a rarer event. If you look at murder-suicide overall, most of the cases are a decision to commit suicide and to take their partner or children with them. It is not a case that they get into a fight, kill the female and, out of remorse, then commit suicide. Remorse doesn't really come into it. Most of it, as far as I can see, is revenge and anger.'

During his work in the UK and also in Australia, Dr Milroy looked at hundreds of cases of murder-suicide and familicide and came up with five clear triggering categories: mental illness, financial stress, elderly infirm, spousal breakdown and criminal activity. 'The latter,' he says, 'are a rarity and involve people taking their lives in order to prevent themselves going into the criminal justice system. It is like the old fashioned term of cheating the hangman. In the studies there were only really one or two who did that. Even when they reached a point that they had decided to commit suicide they were still hell bent on destruction. One had killed police officers and then gone on the run. Only when he was caught did he commit suicide. That is somebody with a criminal background who would commit suicide when he thought he had been caught in the net. They were very different from the other groups.

'Elderly infirm represented couples where one would get ill such that they were not going to recover. The male would decide that everything was coming to an end and kill the wife, then himself. They are very similar to suicide pacts.

'In the category of financial stress, it was a male that killed the whole family after getting into money worries. They are very prevalent in familicide cases. When I classified the mental-illness group, I did so as a pathologist, not a psychiatrist. But we definitely had people who had clearly diagnosed mental illnesses, or were even psychotic. One guy who was acutely psychotic was interviewed by police before being released from jail about other offences. He had a religious mania and kept referring to religious imagery during the whole interview. Then he was released. He went home and killed his wife and child. He then hanged himself. He obviously had a very disordered thought process.

'We also came across a few who were seriously depressed and appeared to kill as an extended suicide. But a lot of it relates to men wanting control and wanting revenge. I had a number of cases where men had left the family and came back to kill their wife. Those who had physically left normally would just return to kill the wife. I had one case where a man left and then came back, travelling from London to the north of England, a distance of 150 miles. He arrived and ordered the son out of the house, then killed his wife and himself.'

It is difficult to sympathise with a child killer. It is even more difficult to sympathise with a person who murders a child when he or she is a parent. But to understand what drives a parent to kill – and it is understanding alone that will ultimately lead to prevention – it is important to put aside prejudices and try to break down the reasons for these dreadful crimes.

Few studies have been done on the phenomenon of familicide but researcher Neil Websdale, a professor of criminal justice at Northern Arizona University, is one of the few experts on it and has just completed a major study, published in the US as *Familicidal Hearts*. In his research of 211 familicide cases, conducted over twelve years, he found that the perpetrators were overwhelmingly male, with females accounting for just five per cent. His research raises several questions, but in particular why familicide is much more prevalent among Caucasians:

African and Native American cultures have a much higher homicide rate in the US than the Caucasian rate. But we don't see that with familicide. Black and Indian races simply don't commit familicide at the same rate as Caucasians and we cannot explain that. All we can do is be suggestive about it, and look at what the predisposing factors might be in the typical nuclear family unit. It is the norm to marry and have two, three children. There is a sense that that is how life should be and that it should be perfect. Surveys all show that Caucasians want to be in that model, the ideal if you like. It is something that is revered, but when people don't obtain it, when it is not perfect, it can be really devastating.

Websdale's theories break down familicidal killers into two distinct groups. The first, which he refers to as 'livid coercive', are violent, controlling partners who have a history of domestic abuse. They use threats, intimidation and violence to coerce their partners. They are also extremely jealous, and feel a great deal of shame or inadequacy about their role as husbands, lovers or fathers.

The second category he calls 'civil reputable': people who are controlled and stoic, often pillars of the community and good providers for their families. To the outside world they appear to be kind and community-minded; they don't let their anger show. While he says these cases are harder to identify, depression is a key sign and they have feelings of shame similar to their 'livid coercive' counterparts. 'Shame' is key to Websdale's explanation of what drives the familicidal killer:

I contend those who commit familicide experience

overwhelmingly intense feelings of shame, fear, anxiety and aggression that literally drive their acts of mass killing. Indeed, the single most important and consistent theme among the familicide cases is the presence of intense shame in the lives of perpetrators, much of it unacknowledged or bypassed. The livid-coercive hearts tend to disguise or mask their shame, deploying violence, hostility and intimidation to do so. Their civil reputable peers are more likely to repress these painful feelings, submerging or sublimating them to the point they assume menacing forms of deep depression and hopelessness.

The primarily working-class livid-coercive hearts temporarily dissipate their shame through their humiliated fury and the act of familicide, perhaps real-ising a fleeting sense of control and pride. In these cases the familicide comprises the end point in a violent, some-times tyrannical relationship where the eventual perpet-rator engages in frantic and obsessive attempts to control a spouse or partner. The sources of their shame vary but the threatened or actual loss of their love object assumes centre stage, producing great anxiety, fear and rage among men typically vulnerable, dependent and often relatively powerless. The mostly middle-class civil-reputable hearts were quiet, subdued, respectable, upstanding citizens, who had not used violence and intimidation in an attempt to control their intimate partners. These perpetrators killed because their lives were spinning out of control and they perceived they faced the threat of bankruptcy, destit-ution, familial dissolution or some other calamity. For most perpetrators, shame stems in large part from their sense they have failed to live up to the dominant modernist ideas about masculinity, and, in a very small number of cases, femininity.

In understanding the complexities of what drives the killer, Websdale urges us to open ourselves to possibilities that may not be apparent at first glance. As in the case of Diarmuid Flood in Wexford, whose actions baffled his family, friends and the wider community, he suggests we look deeper at what first appears to be a perfect family, a perfect provider and a loving father, who inexplicably snapped.

'There are several cases like that in my own study,' he says. 'There is that haunting presence of the inexplicable when it really does seem utterly inexplicable. We looked at a case in Toronto where a woman murdered her husband and two of her four children. She was a twenty-five-year-old with no history of mental illness. When we brought the two families together after the mass killing, and tried to find an explanation, the families could find absolutely nothing that would have remotely hinted at it. But in cases like that, when it does seem that there is no answer, we have to understand that things may not be as they appear from our standpoint. We have to try to look at them from the standpoint of the perpetrator themselves. I have studied plenty of cases where things look to be going mildly awry in someone's life that most people would simply see as a challenge. But these things can be absolutely overwhelming for others. You have to open your mind about it. Plenty of relationships break down, and while it is upsetting, people get on with it. In cases like Mary Keegan's where there doesn't appear to be any major history of mental issues, it is possible that she had a psychotic break for the first time ever – and by psychotic break we mean a complete break with reality. It takes a lot of strength to slit your own throat, so there was certainly a high level of conviction that things were going very, very wrong.'

Arthur McElhill is a classic case of Websdale's livid-coercive individual. Evidence points to him having been a controlling, domineering man, who used physical violence on his partner. He had convictions for two violent sex attacks against women, yet had managed to hide his past to the extent that most of those living in his community found out about it only after he had died. Secretly he had been fuelling his sexual deviances and in the run-up to his appalling crime, his appetite for teenage girls had become insatiable.

In the months before the fire he had begun an affair with one young girl and was trying to groom others. The mother of a girl staying at his house had found out about his past and gone there to challenge him. His house of cards was about to collapse – and his partner was threatening to leave him. Websdale says that McElhill's shame and anger would have been building: 'The threat of being outed would have manifested the shame he felt about who he was. The shame had already manifested itself in his earlier suicide attempts, which are something we always look for in cases of familicide.'

Stephen Byrne and Greg Fox suffered a similar build-up of shame, and the same threat to their role as provider, father and husband. Fox told garda officers that he loved his wife but that she didn't love him and was going to leave him. His attack on her was ferocious and he said he had killed his children because he didn't want them to wake up and see what he had done to their mother. Byrne had had a tense relationship with his wife, Maeve, because of her extra-marital affairs. While he had moved his family to a new home in a bid to start afresh in the months leading up to his crime, he had suspected that she was having another affair and they had spoken of splitting up and possibly divorcing.

Byrne, Fox and McElhill acted in rage and from the intense jealousy surrounding the threat of separation. Interestingly, they also shared a trait found in most mass killers: disconnection from others. Most mass killers and indeed serial killers are loners. While many can form a relationship, they still live an isolated existence where they just can't seem to fit into society. In the scenario of a familicide, the family, tentative as it may be, is their world and most feel a sense of ownership over their wives and children.

Shane Clancy had no family of his own to wipe out but he was driven to a similarly psychotic state by his intense jealousy at the breakdown of his relationship with Jennifer Hannigan. He displayed signs that he felt he owned her, even telling her father that he had been put on earth to love her and that nobody else would love her as much as he did. He had tattooed himself with her name. He had broken up the relationship but immediately regretted his decision and used stalking techniques to monitor and track her movements, including the use of her Facebook site to check her planned activities and any new friends she was making.

Jennifer described how he had 'changed' utterly from the moment she told him about her new relationship with Seb Creane. His murder-suicide rampage was blamed on the anti-depressant he had been prescribed, but it is far more likely that he was driven by a psychosis that had been intensifying in the months since his split from his girlfriend. Following the inquest at which his actions were blamed on the drug, the College of Psychiatry in Ireland initially refused to comment, but later said there was 'no evidence' of a link between anti-depressants and homicide: 'recent' discussion around the risks had been 'speculative' and failed to recognise that untreated depression can have a fatal outcome. While not referring directly to the case, the college added that a link between anti-depressants and violence, with no scientific basis, risked 'a false and stigmatising stereotype' that people living with mental illness were violent. It said it also recognised that, at an individual level, the period early in treatment may be a time of increased risk for suicide, and that all doctors should be aware of this.

For those who seek help, the first line of pharmacological treatment for depressive illness is an SSRI, the very drug group that Shane Clancy's mother insists drove him to kill. But Clancy's worrying behaviour in relation to his former girlfriend far preceded his drug treatment. He had been stalking her, penning bizarre letters to her, and had even shaved his head and grown a beard to look like her new boyfriend. Many who present for psychiatric help often do so when they are well into their mental illness, and Shane Clancy's symptoms appear to many experts as utterly psychotic.

In her book *Psychiatry and Primary Care*, a textbook for GPs, Professor Patricia Casey, Professor of Psychiatry at the Mater Misericordiae University Hospital, UCD says 'common sense' dictates that if there is a real risk of suicide, a doctor should consider admitting a patient to hospital for their own safety. Clancy had attempted to overdose and had slashed his wrists shortly before his attack on the Creane brothers and Jennifer Hannigan. A link between SSRIs and suicide has generally not been substantiated, according to Professor Casey, who cites investigations by the Food and Drug Administration of the United States, the Medicines and Healthcare Products Regulatory Agency in Britain and the Irish Medicines Board along with their European counterparts:

Moreover, the National Institute of Clinical Excellence

(NICE) (2009) in Britain continues to recommend SSRIs as the first line of pharmacological treatment for depressive illness, in those over the age of 18. NICE also recommends that, irrespective of age, those considered to be at increased risk of suicide, for any reason, should be seen every week, once antidepressants have been initiated, until the risk subsides . . . A problem in assessing the causal role of antidepressants in suicide is that simply assuming when a behaviour, such as suicide, follows the use of a particular anti-depressant, one must have caused the other is fallacious since this does not take account of other background factors, prior suicide attempts or the stage in the illness at which the medications are prescribed. Indeed antidepressants are frequently prescribed during a period of deteriorating symptoms with evolving suicidal ideation.

While Leonie Fennell, Shane Clancy's mother, continues her campaign against the drugs, experts would agree that the young man was driven to kill by a jealous rage and a sense of ownership of the girl he had hoped to marry.

Like familicide, murder-suicide is rare, but police in Northern Ireland are currently investigating a case where it is believed a doorman took his own life after killing his wife at their Antrim home: in 2010 Phillip Hull and his wife Sharon had separated just a month before he killed her in their home, then gassed himself in his car. Three years before, Northern Ireland had seen a similar case, in which a husband shot dead his newly-recruited policewoman wife with her own gun, then turned it on himself. Mary Caroline Kewley had just been issued with her firearm when Andrew killed her in August 2007. She wanted to divorce him, and the couple had had rows about how to divide their house.

For Websdale, Diarmuid Flood is a classic case of the civil-reputable offender: middle class, upstanding in his community and not violent towards his wife. He says the case bears many similarities to the family wipe-out by Robert Mochrie in the UK. In 2000 Mochrie had bludgeoned his wife and four children to death, before swallowing a cocktail of slug pellets, weed killer and paracetamol, then hanging himself. Outwardly he had seemed to enjoy a happy and privileged suburban life and there was deep shock when it was learned that he had committed such an appalling act on his own family. He left behind no note or clue as to what had motivated him.

Mochrie had been a wealthy businessman, who lived in a large, expensive home in Cardiff, and had been married for more than twenty years to Catherine, a housewife and mature student. Their eldest son, James, had just won a place at Bristol University to study law; daughter Sian was doing well at school; fourteen-year-old Luke had minor learning difficulties; and Bethan, the youngest, was autistic, attending a special-needs school. Friends later described Mochrie as a quiet, somewhat antisocial man, who was definitely not aggressive.

Behind the scenes and the expensive house, investigators would find that Mochrie was facing bankruptcy, his wife was having an affair and he himself was regularly visiting a prostitute.

It was eleven days before the family were discovered decomposing in their beds where he had beaten and stabbed them to death. Detective Inspector Paul Bethell, who headed the investigation, told the *Guardian* newspaper: 'It was not mayhem or a bloodbath. It's methodical. It's controlled, managed. He's used some degree of pre-planning. Picture the scene. The house is in darkness, the house is silent, and he is walking around. He goes from room to room. He strikes each of them with a blow or blows to the head. He then covers them with the duvet. It's a strange act. Why is he covering them? Downstairs, we found a mop and bucket that had been used to wipe the blood off the wall in one of the rooms. The mopping was a fascinating act. It wasn't the action of someone trying to clean up a crime scene. It was like tidying up. He wasn't trying to conceal anything. It's pointless. What is going through his mind?'

Shame was what was going through his mind, according to Websdale. Mochrie had a lot of secrets and had even hidden a history of depression from his wife, refusing to be admitted to a psychiatric hospital in case she found out about his problems. Mochrie's depression had manifested itself over the years in a number of ways. He had complained of panic attacks and seeing lights. Diarmuid Flood, too, had told a doctor he was having panic attacks, sweating and waking up in the middle of the night. He had also become delusional about his own health problems, believing himself to have a serious illness, although none could be found. He had been referred to a psychiatrist but there is no indication that he had spoken to his wife about his problems: he had kept his mental-health issues hidden from family and friends, to the extent that he would not wait at the health centre if others were there.

In both households, the men and women had defined roles. Neither Mochrie nor Flood was violent to his wife. Both men operated as the provider and were in charge of the family finances. Mochrie was facing financial ruin; Flood certainly believed he was. Unlike Mochrie's, his was a delusional belief. After they died it emerged that the Floods had left an estate valued at more than a million euro. Both Mochrie and Flood killed their families in their beds, in a methodical, well-thought-out way. Flood had obtained a gun and cartridges weeks beforehand. In both cases there is no suggestion that either exploded in rage or had any argument on the night of their crimes. The wives were killed by a blow or bullet meaning there was no suggestion of any sexual rage. There was also no suggestion that either Catherine Mochrie or Lorraine Flood was planning to leave her husband.

If Mochrie and Flood were methodical in carrying out the murder of their families, Adrian Dunne had planned the death of his wife, Ciara, and their two little girls carefully. While the couple had made the Plan for their funeral together, and Dunne's family have insisted that he did not act alone, there are a number of glaring inconsistencies in the suggestion that he and Ciara had formed a suicide pact. First, Dunne portrayed many elements of the classic familicidal killer: he was a controlling loner who isolated his wife, refusing even to allow her to speak to her family on the phone and turning her parents away when they had travelled a great distance to see her. P.J. and Marian O'Brien have maintained a dignified silence about their daughter and have every right to do so. They politely declined a request to be interviewed for this book. It is difficult to ascertain how far Ciara's learning difficulties left her vulnerable to believing a scenario that would be inconceivable to most: that she was planning her daughters' funerals 'just in case'.

However, as the O'Briens were negotiating with the Dunne family about the burial of their daughter and granddaughters, they asked Dr Jim McDaid to give a brief interview about her. He described Ciara as 'a very impressionable woman' and Adrian as a 'domineering' man, who 'isolated' his wife. Ciara was a slow learner and had attended a special-needs school, where she met Adrian, who had been assessed as suffering from a mild mental handicap. Despite his difficulties, he was able to access every social-welfare entitlement for his family. He appeared to move expertly through the system. It is likely that he, rather than Ciara, had cut up the mobile phone Sim cards, rendering them useless for analysis. A forensic scientist who examined them recognised that whoever had done it was forensically aware and cut them up to destroy data stored on them: the act of a clever individual.

Although it is difficult to see how Ciara could have gone along with the funeral plan without knowing what was going to happen, it is important to look at the situation closely. Someone with a higher IQ might have become alarmed that such intricate plans for their death were being made, but it is possible that Ciara simply believed it was nothing more than a precaution. More importantly, if she was part of a 'suicide pact', it is bizarre that she would have agreed to be strangled. Websdale says any insinuation that they had planned their deaths together, like Dunne's suicide text, should be considered with caution: 'It is impossible to know if he was beating her or tyrannising her. But he was certainly isolating her, and the evidence given of how she goes to the gym and he sits outside shows a level of isolation that is very worrying. It is entrapping her and purveying her. It is consistent with what many do in cases of familicide. Dunne had certainly suffered a pained life and had genetic impairments that he had passed on to his own children. Many people lead pained lives and very few go to the extreme of killing, but in this case everything would point to a familicide.'

Like familicide, filicide is a rarely studied and poorly understood phenomenon in Ireland, not least because most filicides also succeed in killing themselves. However, it is known from research carried out in the US and the UK that it is a predominantly female phenomenon. While men usually commit familicide through a sense of ownership of wife and children, women rarely kill their husbands or partners when they choose to kill their child. Ownership stops at the child. Studies have also suggested that women kill more gently – somehow grasping the last straws of their role as protector, as they end the life they bore. Of course there are the exceptions, such as Mary Keegan, whose method of killing her young sons was violent in the extreme. Women tend to kill their children when they are young, and often in the delusional belief that they are protecting them from a future of hardship. Depression is almost always an issue.

Dr Patricia Casey says schizophrenia, psychopathic depression, severe post-natal depression and hypochondriacal delusions are often present when a parent, and particularly a mother, kills: 'Many can have serious hypochondriacal delusions and believe they or their children have very severe illnesses, like cancer. Although they have been to doctors and have been assured they do not, they are still utterly deluded that they are sick or going to die. Children are sometimes killed by their parents, and most commonly this is by a mother suffering with a major mental illness, most commonly psychotic depression, believing, falsely and with absolute conviction, that her child is inhabited by the devil. There can be delusions of poverty, even with people who are wealthy. Some believe that parts of their body are rotting. Often you will find that they have been to GPs and symptoms have been recognised, but nobody is going to imagine that a person is going to end up killing their family or their child. Someone who does that is at the very severe end of a psychotic illness.'

She continues: 'In the past doctors didn't ask about suicide, but now they have got very good at doing that when someone presents with depression or other illnesses. But they are far less likely to talk to someone about homicidal thoughts and that is because it is just so rare. Just how rare it is is shown in a Finnish study, published in 2006, which revealed that of 1,397 suicides, ten were in the homicide-suicide category, most commonly the killing of a partner or spouse followed by suicide of the perpetrator, equivalent to the rate of 0.2 per 100,000 population and, of the latter, only one was familicide.'

According to Professor Casey, those suffering from delusions can often be quite prepared to discuss them in the early stages of the illness. Of them, most can be successfully treated with a stay in hospital, with or without psychiatric drugs: 'Most serious mental illness can be treated, but it is getting a person into treatment on time that can be a key to avoiding these situations. There will be signs there. Someone would likely be losing weight, not sleeping, appear dishevelled, and they would be acting very out of character and bizarre. There will be those who harbour the delusions, but many will openly attempt to have something done about them, as is the case of those with hypochondriacal delusions. I once had a patient who was convinced that his knees were rotting. He had been checked out and there was nothing wrong with him, but he was totally deluded about it. Illnesses like puerperal post-natal depression are very treatable but very dangerous. Often those who have it would believe their baby is possessed with the devil and would be likely to harm the child. If a person is having delusions, it is very important for them to see a psychiatrist who has experience in how to deal with it.'

'In most cases of filicide, you will see that these women are very, very seriously disturbed and most likely at the end point of a severe mental illness. This is not just a woman experiencing a tough time, these are often women who are completely psychotic and delusional and need to be hospitalised.'

In *Psychiatry in Primary Care*, Professor Casey highlights the fact that the majority of psychiatric conditions initially present in a GP's surgery. It can be challenging to recognise and diagnose mental illness accurately. She considers the rising rate of suicide among women:

> The rising suicide rate in women may also be a result of the anomie process whereby women have moved from a traditional albeit restrictive role to a broader and more diverse pattern of behaviour and functioning. Current approaches to measuring anomie focus on social fragmentation and material deprivation although the former seems to have a greater impact than the latter ... A further theory – the egoistic theory – views social isolation as being of significance and may explain the high suicide rate in cities, in migrants and in those who are divorced, widowed and single. The role of loneliness and isolation has been confirmed in observational studies.

Loneliness and isolation might indeed have played a part in the cases of Sharon Grace, Catriona Innes and Eileen Murphy, all struggling single mums trying to work and rear their children.

Dr Chris Milroy's studies have found that women often kill their children as part of their own plan to die and successfully carry it out due to their own dedication to ending their lives: 'When women kill their children it is often like an extended suicide and you will often find they were very depressed,' he says. 'When women kill their partner they usually do it as a type of a delayed self-defence. They will wait until a drunken, abusive partner is passed out and then kill them. Men will regularly kill their partner and then commit suicide, but women rarely do that. But when they kill a child, it is like it is part of their own suicide. Women tend to be more passive when they kill children. While men will turn a gun on them or strangle them, women tend to smother or poison them. In my experience it is nearly always an extended suicide. When a woman makes the decision to commit suicide, she thinks the child would be better off dead, too, than trying to cope without her. When men kill their children, there tends to be revenge in the equation. It's like they're saying: "If I can't have them, no one can."'

Experts tend to agree that women who kill their children often have a recognised mental illness and that many are suffering from a severe form of post-natal depression.

A study on filicide, conducted in 1969 by the American Professor Philip J. Resnick, is still cited by experts today who rely on his typology of filicides. *Child Murder By Parents: A Psychiatric Review of Filicide* examines 131 cases of parents who murdered their children, then attempted, successfully or not, suicide. Of the sample, eighty-eight mothers had killed and forty-three fathers. The study found that the most dangerous period for victims was in their first six months of life, when a suicidal mother was more likely to think of a baby as a possession and feel inseparable from him or her.

Head trauma, strangulation and drowning were the most common causes of death of a child, while the study found that mothers tended to drown, suffocate or gas their children while men stabbed, squeezed or hit them. In a case that stood out for Resnick, a father placed his son on a drill press and drilled a hole through the child's heart.

As in more modern studies of filicide, the leading diagnosis for a mother who had killed a child was schizophrenia, while a father was found to be mostly non-psychotic. Depression was also noted in 71 per cent of mothers – twice that of fathers.

Resnick's typology of filicides was broken down into five distinct categories. What he termed 'Altruistic filicide'was totally associated with suicide: a parent felt they couldn't abandon their children when they killed themselves. In some cases, filicide was intended to relieve suffering; in many cases the suffering was found to be delusional, and the findings suggest that a parent often killed a child in an effort to prevent the children being taken by 'paranoid persecutors'.

In 'acutely psychotic filicide', a parent killed when under the influence of hallucinations, epilepsy or delirium. Resnick admitted that this was his weakest typology, as it included those cases in which no comprehensible motive could be ascertained. Explanations offered included theories relating to a short circuit in the brain or cataclysmic mental crisis in the perpetrator. Both occur when an impulse is translated into a violent action. Although the category is the weakest, it would explain why Mary Keegan, a loving mother, suddenly and without warning stabbed her two little boys to death, then killed herself. At her inquest, it was explained that she had become deluded about impoverishment.

Resnick's third category was 'unwanted-child filicide', in which a parent simply no longer wants their child. The fourth group, 'accidental', was usually the result of battered-child syndrome, and the study found that it involved more men than women. Finally, Resnick cited 'spouse revenge', in which a child is killed in a deliberate attempt to make a spouse suffer.

Websdale and Milroy believe that Chris Crowley fits the 'spouse revenge' category. 'He was evidently controlling, dominant and domineering. And that is one of the hallmarks of all these cases. He would have been able to dominate the young girl he had the affair with and also the child. He would have felt shame about getting caught out with the child and called to account for his actions of the eighteen months before her death. There is a humiliated fury there when he shoots the little girl in the face, but he is getting back at the mother out of a need, as a man, to be revered. When the police arrive at the door he is clearly in trouble. All his control is gone so it's game up. He kills the daughter to get back at the wife for the way in which he feels she has ruined his life,' says Websdale.

Resnick's study found that after an altruistic or actively psychotic case of filicide there is often a release from tension, which, he says, may explain the failure of some parents to complete their crime or their suicide. 'The murderer may appear dazed or confess in a mechanical way. They will usually make no attempt to conceal the crime.' Greg Fox is a case in point. When gardaí arrived at his home in Westmeath where he had beaten and stabbed his wife to death and also stabbed his two little boys, he was able mechanically to tell officers why he had done it. He told them that his wife Debbie didn't love him and was going to leave him. And he said he had killed the boys because he didn't want them to wake up and see what he had done to their mother.

On the other hand, those in the categories of unwanted child or accidental filicide can go to great lengths to conceal what they have done. Interestingly, the study also found that while fathers who survived were more likely to be executed or sent to prison, mothers usually ended up in hospital. In the study group, 75 per cent had shown psychiatric symptoms and some mothers had talked openly about suicide, expressing concern for their children's future. Lynn Gibbs had done both. She realised she had suicidal thoughts and had become obsessed with her daughter Ciara's anorexia. Another 40 per cent of the study group had been seen by psychiatrists or physicians shortly before their crimes. Arthur McElhill, Diarmuid Flood and Nollaig Owen had all seen doctors before they died. Resnick's study urges those in the medical profession who see potentially suicidal people to ask them direct questions about their feelings for their children.

Professor Casey says: 'Most murders by parents are in the context of mental illness, depression, drug abuse or schizophrenia. Or they may be an impulsive act of revenge, arising from something like a marital dispute. This has been recorded and written about in psychiatric literature for years. It is not just a phenomenon of recent decades sadly, it's a tragic feature of life. When delusional thoughts occur, such parents can often believe that taking their child's life is an act of love. If drug abuse is involved, they tend to be so intoxicated that they may not realise they are killing a human being. When there are marital problems, it is often a question of reaching for the nearest and most vulnerable object. Unfortunately, that is frequently the children.

'You can understand why people may have no sympathy for a child-killer, but it should always be remembered that it generally occurs in the context of psychological problems. It is not something that is carried out in cold blood, except in very, very rare instances.'

Nollaig Owen certainly had a recognised psychiatric disorder when she pushed her baby Tadgh into a river and killed herself. She had been diagnosed with post-natal depression, a psychiatric illness that can develop during pregnancy and childbirth. In a paper recently published in the *Irish Journal of Psychological Medicine*, Veronica O'Keane criticised Ireland's lack of planning in perinatal psychiatric services. She pointed out that, although Ireland has the highest birth rate in the EU, the services have not been planned strategically. 'Psychiatry should lead the way in convincing health-service managers of the need to address the psychological as well as the medical needs of pregnant women. Perhaps the most compelling argument for this need is that suicide is now the leading cause of maternal death in the UK.'

In recent years, researchers have been looking at genes, which can make women more vulnerable to severe mental illness after childbirth. Post-partum psychosis is one of the most severe forms of mental illness, and brings with it an increased risk of suicide. It is not the same illness as post-natal depression and comes on within a few days of giving birth. Also known as puerperal psychosis, it can take the form of mania, severe depression and delusions, confusion or mood swings. It can make it difficult for a woman to bond with her baby. There is some evidence that the condition may run in families and it is slightly more common in first pregnancy. It is treated in hospitals with anti-psychotic drugs or anti-depressants and recovery may take months.

After the death of Nollaig Owen and her baby boy, the Irish Association of Suicidology released a statement about the recent spate of suicides by parents who had also killed their children:

> Murder suicide including murder filicide, which is the murder of a child by one or other parent who subsequently ends their own life by suicide, though rare, is more common than one might think and always a matter of great concern. The incidence of murder-suicide when statistics are examined over the years is in the region of one per 500,000 to 750,000 of the

population per annum. These events are thought to be under-reported. The parent in these cases is more commonly the father than the mother according to international research. Factors leading to these deaths are numerous and include postpartum depression, perinatal psychosis, major depressive illness, other major psychiatric illness, relationship problems, loneliness, hopelessessness and helplessness.

The IAS criticised the lack of specialist psychiatric services for women during pregnancy and the year following birth, and the lack of proper risk assessment for children:

Many of the psychiatric services are remote, not user-friendly and not always readily accessible. The provision of psychiatric and counselling services is unevenly spread throughout the country. There is need for greater funding of all these services and for the voluntary organisations that are making such valuable contributions to all aspects of suicide prevention and support for the bereaved at both national and local levels.

Aware, the charity that aims to defeat depression, also issued a guide for mothers and their families on post-natal depression. Puerperal psychosis, it said, is rare, but affects one in every 500 mothers. It is a biological or chemical form of mood disorder similar to manic depression. It warned that a mother who is very depressed can harbour strong suicidal ideas or, although less frequently, an impulse to kill their child.

Sharon Grace and Catriona Innes harboured such strong feelings. Sharon Grace's parents said that when they arrived at her house just hours before she would walk into the sea and drown her little girls, she had been crying and was very upset. She had been going downhill since the question of custody of the children had been raised by social workers after she had denied her ex-husband Barry access to them. Catriona Innes had told friends and family that she was finding life hard. On the night she smothered Caitlin and then hanged herself, she had told her mother that she was 'fed up'. She also made a call to an ex-boyfriend, which went unanswered.

While many cases can be categorised in the typology put forward by the experts, some do not fit in so easily. Despite a general acceptance that alcohol is rarely found to be a direct cause of filicide, Ruth Murphy had consumed a considerable amount when she drowned her young son, Karl. However, she also had serious custody issues surrounding the little boy that related to her alcoholism.

Over recent years, a number of high-profile cases in Ireland of the death of families or children have led to calls for full inquiries. The McElhill and Dunne tragedies led to detailed reports focusing on the families' relationship with Social Services. When Sharon Grace looked for help at the eleventh hour before walking her daughters into the sea, she had asked for a social worker but was told no one was available because it was the weekend.

Professor Casey believes that the report's focus on the intervention of social workers is a waste of time, as parents in psychosis need psychiatric help: 'I have to admit I find it incredible that in trying to work out what went wrong in some of these cases, the whole focus has been on social workers and their intervention in the family. It is obvious that it is not social work that would help in these cases but psychiatric help, and it seems to be a waste of time and money to commission reports focused solely on the wrong thing. If these reports are done, they should be more focused on mental health and psychiatry.'

In April 2010, in Northern Ireland, two health trusts apologised for 'inexcusable failures' surrounding the treatment of a suicidal woman who killed her young daughter and herself. Madeline O'Neill smothered nine-year-old Lauren after telling health professionals she had thought about ending their lives and had checked the internet for methods to do so. In a joint statement, the Belfast Health and Social Care Trust and Western Health and Social Care Trust accepted that Lauren's death should not have occurred.

The apology and an admission of negligence formed part of the settlement of two civil actions, one taken by Madeline's estranged husband and the father of Lauren, John O'Neill, and the other by Madeline's family. At the time John O'Neill had no idea she had indicated she might harm Lauren, and only found out about it when police were investigating their deaths and retrieved her medical notes.

Madeline had developed an acute psychiatric illness two months before she killed her daughter and herself; she was treated as an in- and out-patient. The statement said:

> During the course of her treatment Madeline O'Neill made disclosures to some of those treating her that she intended to take her own life and that of Lauren O'Neill. The Belfast Health and Social Care Trust and the Western Health and Social Care Trust accept that there was a failure to act properly or appropriately on these disclosures so as to ensure that all relevant arrangements were put in place for the protection of Lauren. They further accept that there was a failure to inform John O'Neill of the content of any of these

disclosures at any time prior to Lauren's death with the consequence that John O'Neill, at no time, had any knowledge or reason to suspect that the life of his daughter was at risk. The trusts accept that these failures were inexcusable and resulted in Lauren being left exposed to the foreseeable risk of harm from Madeline, who remained psychiatrically unwell.

Northern Ireland's Senior Coroner, John Leckey, said the case was of major public interest. 'What I find particularly upsetting is the death of a nine-year-old girl,' he said. 'I'm pleased that the trusts have recognised the dreadful fate that befell her and have put in place procedures that hopefully will prevent a recurrence of anything remotely similar.'

The crowd who stand outside the church in Ballycotton in County Cork are silent. All that can be heard is the church bells and the crunch of car tyres on a frozen road. Then it appears: the hearse bearing two white coffins, one smaller than the other. Two sisters, two children, who should have been breathing in fresh air this cold November day, who should have been looking upon the beautiful bay that sparkles clear and blue. Two little girls who should have been wearing hats and gloves; who should have had clean tissues tucked up their sleeves; who should have been wearing their new winter boots; who should have felt a warm kiss on their faces. Their father must have been so proud on the days when they were born. He must have loved them beyond any love he could ever have thought imaginable. Yet he chose to bring their lives to a premature end, aged just two and six. Ella and Zoë, frozen for ever in time. Gone. And everyone wants to know why.

ACKNOWLEDGEMENTS

A special word of thanks is due to all those who contributed to the research of this book, most of whom will have to remain nameless. You know who you are and I really appreciate your insight and your invaluable work investigating these tragic cases. And of course, thanks for the coffee.

Utmost gratitude to the experts who gave me their time and experience in the intricate understanding of what drives these killers. Thanks to Professor of Psychiatry Patricia Casey of University College Dublin; Neil Websdale, Professor of Criminal Justice at Northern Arizona University and the Director and Principal Project Advisor of the National Domestic Violence Fatality Review Initiative at the US Department of Justice; and Chris Milroy, Professor of Forensic Pathology at Ottawa Hospital in Canada.

Thanks to the work of Professor Jack Levin of the North Eastern University in Boston and to Professor Philip J Resnick of University Hospitals of Cleveland, one of the earliest academics whose work I studied for this book. And to the countless others who have tried to make sense of why these dreadful crimes happen.

To all my fellow journalists who have reported on the cases contained in this book; who have awkwardly stood in freezing cemeteries trying desperately not to intrude on grief, who have been pilloried for reporting the truth and who have had to dig deep to try to make sense of how a normal person can be responsible for the most abnormal of crimes. Every word you have written, every observation you have made is part of a great tapestry of understanding which we need to prevent the slaughter of the innocents. Of course this book could never have been written without the support and encouragement from all my colleagues on Ireland's best newspaper. In particular a big thanks to Pictures Editor Owen Breslin for trawling through our vast archives without complaint, our wonderful backbench of Brian Farrell and Finn Gillespie for doing their damndest to make me look good, the Consigliere; Kieran Kelly for all the advice and of course to Gerry Lennon, Colm MacGinty and Neil Leslie for captaining the good ship Sunday World and all who sail in her.

Finally to Ciara Considine and Breda Purdue of Hachette Books Ireland for tackling this subject.

Nicola Tallant, March 2011.

Picture acknowledgements

The publishers would like to thank the *Sunday World*, Provision, Kobpix, Arthur Carron/Collins, Collect/PA, Niall Carson/PA, PA Wire, PJ Browne, and John Walsh for kind permission to reproduce images on the cover and inside pages of the book.